PRAISE FOR *MILLION DOLLAR* ...RD

"Lori Culwell's insight has made DiscoverNursing.com the award-winning website it is today. This book is an invaluable resource for anyone with a small business."

—ANDREA HIGHAM, Director, Johnson & Johnson
Campaign for Nursing's Future

"I have known and worked with Lori Culwell for six years on numerous Internet-related projects. I have been involved in the Internet since the early days and have found her talent, vision, and expertise invaluable. If an old Internet veteran like me listens to her, you should, too."

—STEVE HAUBER, Publisher and CEO,
Gannett Healthcare Group

"Whether building your website from scratch or improving the performance of your current site, *Million Dollar Website* provides a thorough look at the world of website building and marketing and is a terrific resource. It is an insightful road map of best practices and a remarkably useful book for businesses. Lori Culwell has done it again."

—SCOTT SCHNEIDER, EVP and Managing Director,
Ruder Finn Interactive

# Million Dollar Website

Simple Steps to Help
You Compete with the
Big Boys—Even on a
Small Business Budget

## Lori Culwell

**PRENTICE HALL PRESS**

PRENTICE HALL PRESS
Published by the Penguin Group
Penguin Group (USA) Inc.
375 Hudson Street, New York, New York 10014, USA
Penguin Group (Canada), 90 Eglinton Avenue East, Suite 700, Toronto, Ontario M4P 2Y3, Canada (a division of Pearson Penguin Canada Inc.) • Penguin Books Ltd., 80 Strand, London WC2R 0RL, England • Penguin Group Ireland, 25 St. Stephen's Green, Dublin 2, Ireland (a division of Penguin Books Ltd.) • Penguin Group (Australia), 250 Camberwell Road, Camberwell, Victoria 3124, Australia (a division of Pearson Australia Group Pty. Ltd.) • Penguin Books India Pvt. Ltd., 11 Community Centre, Panchsheel Park, New Delhi—110 017, India • Penguin Group (NZ), 67 Apollo Drive, Rosedale, North Shore 0632, New Zealand (a division of Pearson New Zealand Ltd.) • Penguin Books (South Africa) (Pty.) Ltd., 24 Sturdee Avenue, Rosebank, Johannesburg 2196, South Africa

Penguin Books Ltd., Registered Offices: 80 Strand, London WC2R 0RL, England

While the author has made every effort to provide accurate telephone numbers and Internet addresses at the time of publication, neither the publisher nor the author assumes any responsibility for errors, or for changes that occur after publication. Further, the publisher does not have any control over and does not assume any responsibility for author or third-party websites or their content.

First edition: May 2009

Library of Congress Cataloging-in-Publication Data

Culwell, Lori.
    Million dollar website : simple steps to help you compete with the big boys—even on a small business budget / Lori Culwell.
        p. cm.
Includes index.
ISBN 978-0-7352-0441-6
1. Internet marketing. 2. Electronic commerce 3. Websites—Design. I. Title.
HF5415.1265.C855 2009
658.8'72—dc22                                  2009005520

PRINTED IN THE UNITED STATES OF AMERICA

10 9 8 7 6 5 4 3 2 1

Most Prentice Hall Press books are available at special quantity discounts for bulk purchases for sales promotions, premiums, fund-raising, or educational use. Special books, or book excerpts, can also be created to fit specific needs. For details, write: Special Markets, Penguin Group (USA) Inc., 375 Hudson Street, New York, New York 10014.

*For Stephan, and for The Rose*

# Acknowledgments

First and foremost, a huge thank-you to Stephan Cox, my husband, best friend, and partner in crime. None of this would be possible without you! Thanks for helping me work through ideas, proposals, drafts, and chapters, and for being generally awesome. Thanks to Dave Dunton for being a great agent—one with whom I hope to keep working for many years to come. And let us not forget about Maria! Maria Gagliano, editor extraordinaire, whose excellent ideas shaped and molded this book into something better than even I thought it could be. Thank you as well to the many smart work colleagues over the years who have enhanced my knowledge of websites, usability, marketing, branding, design, and everything else you see here. These include, but are certainly not limited to, Andrea, Lorie, Owen, Amit, Crystal, Lee, Prayag, Scott, Brad, Bonin, Chris, Guy, Leslie, Julie, Megan, Nadia, Vince, Julie, Jenn, Jason, Larry, and Nancy.

# Contents

# Introduction
## How to Make Your Website Compete with the Big Boys

**I started thinking** about writing this book one day while I was waiting to get something copied at Kinko's. I was standing in line behind a woman who was ordering reprints of a promotional flyer for her business—a retreat for older, single women. She kept saying to the Kinko's guy, "I need more people to go to my website. Not enough people are finding my site, and when they do, they're not signing up for my seminars."

I didn't want to pry, but she seemed at wit's end, and so finally I introduced myself, explaining that I was a web consultant who helped Fortune 500 companies develop and improve their websites. We talked briefly about her site, and then I got the address and agreed to take a look at it for her. I'm not the kind of person who bad-mouths other people, so let's just say her site lacked a clear focus . . . and was really outdated. Even if her seminars/retreats were the best thing since sliced bread, it didn't matter, because her website wasn't compelling enough to get people to sign up, or even to investigate further.

She clearly had made the site herself (good for her!), and although it did have many of the elements a good site needs (including interesting content about her company and the retreats), it did not have several important elements. For one, there was no clear navigational structure, a must-have for directing customers to the many different types of information on the site. For another, there was no way to pay for the seminars and trips online. There was no privacy policy and no way to capture email addresses for follow-up and future marketing purposes, and the company contact information was hard to find and incomplete. Plus, the site was very, very pink, which I thought some potential customers might find a little off-putting. While the woman claimed that her target audience was women age fifty to sixty-five, the pink was reminiscent of Barbie, and was more appropriate to a much younger, "tween" age group. The color alone might have been driving potential customers away.

What was this business owner to do? She really couldn't afford to hire an experienced web consultant to tell her how to improve her site. She certainly couldn't afford a team of Internet experts to actually revamp the site: an information architect to perfect the structure; a designer to make it look and feel better; a writer to set the tone, to make sure the content has enough of the right keywords so that search engines will find the site, and to consistently add interesting content; and a marketing specialist to position and promote the site properly.

That's when I got to thinking. . . . The Internet, being "the great equalizer" that it is, should not be about the "haves" and "have nots." Small businesses and independent contractors that create and maintain their own sites should have access to good information about what works and what doesn't when it comes to websites. They shouldn't have to pay a team of experts $100,000 for a redesign of their sites, or even $1,000 for a consultant like me to tell them what's wrong and how to fix it themselves.

But if you can't afford to hire a professional web team or an experienced consultant, how do you get the expertise required to create a site that does what you need for it to do? As I thought about this common dilemma, it occurred to me that anyone should be able to get information about the best available tools and strategies for creating and marketing a website . . . from an experienced expert, and all in one place. You, starting right where you are, should be able to build and grow a "million dollar website," without the million dollar price tag.

This book is just that—a guide to improving your website, based on my eleven years of experience working on websites for big companies.

In order to successfully compete for your share of the vast and growing online markets, your site must do and have certain things. These website "essentials" are the same no matter how big or small your business. The features and functionality that customers need and want from a large corporation's site are the same as what they need and want from your site. The e-commerce marketing strategies that work for the big guys' sites will work equally well for yours. There is no reason why your business's website cannot be as successful as that of a much bigger enterprise. You just need the same information and tools that are available to them, and then your site will have the strength and power of the million dollar website, eventually becoming one in its own right (if that's what you want, of course). Depending on your goals for your business and the amount of time you have to spend on your site, it's actually simple to employ a set of tools that will allow your business not only to compete with the big budget, big name sites, but to grow exponentially.

Before we go further, I'd like to take this opportunity to emphasize that this is a guide to *improving your site* . . . and not only a guide to increasing traffic to your site, which is the main (or sole) focus of so many other books on websites. Yes, a huge amount of traffic can be great for your business, but only if the destination you are directing people to is a well-designed, interesting, and usable website. Otherwise, you've wasted money on search engine placement, Google AdWords, or whatever marketing vehicles you've used (and paid for) to drive traffic to your site. One hundred people who actually enjoy and use a properly developed site are much more valuable to you than ten thousand people who get to your site but haven't a clue what the site is about or what to do there.

The quality of the customers' experience beats quantity of traffic every time. Though quality takes more attention to detail, it is what leads to sales and keeps you around in the long run. With Internet commerce, you want a steadily increasing stream of loyal, happy users who return again and again and who recommend your site to others. What you don't want are millions of disappointed, frustrated, or angry people who visit your site once and never come back. Sure, quantity is important, but it is easy enough to build traffic—once (and only if and when) your site is ready for public scrutiny. Nothing sticks in people's minds quite like a poorly designed website. If your site isn't of the quality it needs to be, you really don't want the whole World Wide Web to see it.

Once your website is in good shape, you will find that your sales will improve exponentially, and you will be that much closer to your million dollar website. Not only is your site your company's "face to the world," it is also a primary, and sometimes the only, interface with your customers. When visitors to your site are pleased with their online experience and when they can easily navigate and complete transactions on your site, you will see an increase in both new customers and repeat customers.

This book will help you make simple changes to your website that will enhance users' experience, entice them to purchase your products, and encourage them to come back to your site for frequent return visits . . . and purchases. If you are like most small business owners or managers, your interests and professional experience are in the products you are selling or the content you are providing on your site—and not in the intricacies of online marketing and website usability. Chances are, too, that you are already wearing several hats and have more on your daily to-do list than you could ever hope to complete. So, you might well be wondering, how am I supposed to learn all this web stuff and implement it while doing my regular job and running my business? Good question.

Assuming that you have a few hours per week to work on your website and on your online marketing, this book can show you how to upgrade your site and increase its effectiveness with tools that are readily available to you right now. Whether you created your site yourself or paid someone else to build it for you, there are many simple things you can do to improve your online business, starting today.

There are several ways to use this book, and the goal at all times is for you to be comfortable and not overwhelmed. So there are different ways to do this—the "all in one sitting" way, or the "piece by piece" way. Either one can (and has) worked for my clients, and either one will work for you. Even if you pick up this book at random intervals and flip to a section, you will find something that will help improve your site a little bit. These little changes will make a big difference, and before long you'll be motivated to do more and more.

If you're a "let's begin at the beginning" type of person, then pull up a chair, get out a pen and paper, start with Chapter 1, and let's dive right in. Personally, I think everyone should read Part 1, because all of the things we're going to put into practice on your site are based on the concepts there: fundamentals of good usability, defining your target audience, and knowing your keywords. In Part 2 we'll do a little research and discovery, where you assess your site, locate some facts, and look at some other successful sites to see what they're doing right. If you have a site that's up and running now, we'll also go over how to do some testing to see if it's working, and put some simple changes in place that could make a big change right now. In Part 3 we'll roll up our sleeves and do the work on your site—covering how to reconstruct (or construct, as the case may be) your material for the best usability, the best and clearest designs, and (perhaps most important) the words on your site, both the copywriting and the keyword content. Finally, in Part 4, we'll talk marketing, with surefire strategies, from search engines to newsletters to social networking and everything in between, to get your new site out to the world.

But, like I said, "piece by piece" will work too. Maybe you're totally happy with your site and are just interested in marketing strategies. If that's the case, go directly to Part 4, and save Parts 1 through 3 for if you ever need a redesign or need to know how to get opinions from your customer base. Maybe you're up to your ears in research, and are chomping at the bit to get started on your redesign. Great! Start at Part 3, and read Part 1 for good measure, just to make sure you're firm on the basics. If you don't have a lot of time (and many people with small businesses do not), just check out the contents page to see which concept is most applicable to you, and start there. I promise, you'll never get lost in the technology; we're just having a basic discussion about common sense, with some technology thrown in for good measure. You can do this! My job is just to help you get there.

# The Big Picture

**B**efore **we go** in and start making changes to your site, it will be helpful for you to know a few things about the Internet in general, and what constitutes an effective website. We'll talk about the "user experience" and why it's so important, take a stab at defining your target audience (that is, who's going to be using your website most of the time), and dive into your keyword list, which, believe it or not, is going to be one of the most important tools in the success of your site. Be sure you have a computer with Internet access close by, because we're going to refer to many real-life examples of what works and what doesn't. Before this section is over, you will have taken a look at your own site as if you were seeing it for the first time, which hopefully will give you some ideas of what you need to change. Plus, you'll meet Bob, my fictional website makeover client, whose online dog biscuit store will provide a real-life example of the concepts we're discussing.

# 1 | What Makes a Good Website?

Everything about your website—from the way it looks to the way it works—must meet the quality standards of your target market.

Once upon a time, it was enough to promote your business through advertising, marketing materials, public relations, and word of mouth. Then came the Internet, which added a powerful new must-have weapon to the strategic marketing arsenal. Problem was, very few companies actually knew how to use the web to promote their businesses, and their online marketing strategy, if they had one at all, was often nothing more than trial and error. In fact, until about ten years ago, it was not unusual for a business to have no online presence.

My, how times have changed. Today, having a website is as necessary to your business as having a phone number. And while a good website can greatly enhance your business, a bad site can seriously hurt your bottom line.

A good website can:

▸ Create a positive image and/or distinctive brand for your business
▸ Save you thousands of dollars in marketing materials and direct mailing costs
▸ Generate sales and business contacts round the clock, twenty-four hours a day, seven days a week

▶ Expand your businesses' reach internationally and exponentially

On the other hand, a bad website can:

▶ Reflect poorly on your business image and/or brand
▶ Increase your marketing and sales costs
▶ Limit your marketing reach and distribution channels
▶ Cause customer dissatisfaction and attrition

The good news is that it is not difficult to create a good website or to make a not-so-good website great. Here are the basics you will need to make over your website:

1. A basic understanding of what makes a site work
2. A clear picture of where your site is now (performance statistics, user feedback, sales info, etc.)
3. An idea of where you'd like the site to go (to increase traffic, sales, visit length; to build a mailing list; etc.)
4. A working knowledge of a basic HTML program like Dreamweaver, HomeSite, or FrontPage, funds to hire someone to do the HTML programming for you, or the willingness to try one of the all-inclusive website-building programs like GoDaddy's WebSite Tonight (www.godaddy.com), Intuit's Homestead (www.homestead.com), or one of the templates offered by TypePad or a Mac.com account. Really, with good usability and content, you don't need to be too technical, though the more you can get in and manipulate the code, the more work you can do. I've seen a site built with a TypePad template grow exponentially and sell for seven figures. So don't let lack of technical knowledge make you feel like you can't do this. Not true!

\* \* \*

# So . . . What Makes a Good Website?

This is the million dollar question . . . with a relatively simple answer. It all boils down to a concept called the "user experience," which is basically Internet jargon for "How easy is the website to use?" Are visitors able to find what they're looking for and to do the business they've come for quickly and easily? Is the site missing anything crucial? Might any of the content turn off or alienate your target audience? Is there anything about the structure or usability that might confuse or frustrate users? Do visitors come away well informed and excited about your brand and with a positive impression of your business?

Clearly, many factors contribute to the quality of the user experience. When evaluating the user-experience rating of your site, consider the following:

▶ Who are my ideal users (also known as the primary audience or target market)?
▶ When they get to my site, can they "get" it—what my site is about and what it offers them—within the first five seconds?
▶ Can they quickly and easily tell what I want them to do?
▶ Do I make it easy for them to do it?
▶ Is all of the content useful, enjoyable, and memorable to visitors? Are the site's layout and graphics attractive and appropriate? Is the text interesting, engaging, relevant, and complete?
▶ Is the look and feel of the site distinctive? Does it complement my product/service, my overall business, and the market? Does it enhance or reinforce my brand?
▶ Most important, is the users' overall experience at my site so intuitive, seamless, and positive that they'll keep coming back, again and again?

If you answered no to any of these critical questions, this book will help you make simple changes that will improve the user experience of your website, make visitors love your site as well as the products or services you sell, and hopefully make your site a destination rather than something users must endure in order to get what they came to your site for. You'll be surprised at how much a few subtle changes to your site can increase your sales.

## Tough Love: Getting Real About Your Site

Think of this book as the equivalent of a personal trainer for your website. Its purpose is to help you whip your site into shape. I assume you're reading this book because you're ready to do exactly that. I also assume that what you're looking for is increased traffic and sales, not just compliments. People can say all the nice stuff about your site they want, but the facts are in the stats. When your site is fit for online business, you'll see more action from your site, in terms of both higher traffic and increased sales. That requires taking a good, long, and objective look at your site.

As you go about the process of evaluating and revamping your site—and, for that matter, afterward, as you maintain and upgrade it—I recommend that you solicit the honest opinions of people who have at least a working knowledge of both your business and the Internet. To make your online presence as strong as possible, you need informed and candid feedback, not just a pat on the back.

You also need to be realistic and objective in assessing your current site (if you have one) and what you have in mind for your new or improved site. Right now, get out a pen and paper, and open up your site. Without navigating around or thinking about it too much, write down your first impressions. Now, go through the site as though you were visiting it for the first time, checking out all the different features and functions, and write down notes on your impressions and on what works and what doesn't. Be specific, and try to be objective, as if viewing the site through the eyes of a first-time visitor who has no prior knowledge of or experience with your business. Don't even think about the time and money it took to get your site to where it is today; think only about how your customers and potential customers might see and use your site. If you were a new customer seeing your website for the first time, what would you think? Would it knock your socks off? Would you be able to find your star product? Would you be impressed by the design? Would you "get" it right away; would you understand the point of the site and what you could do there? Or would you be confused disoriented, or even offended by the bad design and then forget why you came to the site, and leave to find a better one? Would you be able to successfully complete a transaction without getting frustrated or hitting a dead end?

In short, does the entire site provide a seamless and satisfying user experience?

If not, why not? Does the site seem too busy and crowded? Does it take too long to load? Do any of the links not work? Is it difficult to navigate from one window or page to another? Is the shopping cart or order form hard to use? Are there any typos or stray graphics? Does it have any unnecessary, unwieldy, or annoying bells and whistles, like a fancy Flash intro or some aggressive pop-up ads? All of these things have driven away users from the biggest-name corporate sites out there—from auto manufacturers to pharmaceutical companies to international banks.

If you feel that you cannot answer these questions and evaluate your site objectively or that you need additional feedback, ask a few knowledgeable friends, family members, and/or colleagues to check out your site. Have them write down their honest opinions of your site—anonymously, if necessary. Tell them to specify what they liked and didn't like, what worked and didn't work for them.

If you don't think your close relationships will survive an analysis of this kind, and you have a budget for your redesign, then you might want to spend a few hundred dollars on a focus group or some simple usability testing. This will tell you what people really think of your site and give you a clear direction. For more information on this, go to Chapter 6.

So . . . how user-friendly is your website? If your site is of the confusing and frustrating variety, don't despair. Remember, the first step toward excellence in anything is determining what needs to be improved. Now I am going to give you some practical tools to do just that—to help you make your site a lean, mean, user-friendly machine. Just by doing this exercise, you've learn the most important part of good web design and development: to think like the user.

\* \* \*

# The User Always Rules

An important thing to remember is that your website is a tool—which someone (the user) actually *uses* to accomplish a task, whether that is to buy something or simply to access the site's content. The number one goal of any website should be to make sure that all users can find what they're looking for and accomplish their objectives without any hassle.

It is also important for each step of the entire online process to be transparent to the user. If the user needs a bunch of directions and cues to make your site work, it's not really working. As we said at the agency where I used to work: "If it needs a sign, it's bad design." When designing and organizing your site, always do so with the user in mind. That's what this book is about. As you learn more about this topic, you will no doubt discover that many of the sites you come across on the Internet were obviously not designed with the user in mind. Some of these sites might have beautiful designs and feature super-duper technology, which is all well and good—but that zing doesn't mean a thing if the site doesn't function properly. Remember: function first, form second—or, put another way, users first, personal style second.

Sounds simple, right? Well, it is . . . and it isn't. Every user is different, and you can't please everyone, but you do want to please the users that make up your target market. So you'll want to identify those users and define their needs, and then tailor your website to fit them.

The bottom line: A website that's built and maintained with the user in mind is more likely to attract the right visitors and to turn them into return customers. Make it easy for them to navigate your site, to find things, to complete transactions and feel good while they're doing it, and you'll win the advantage over your competition. Combine this with a strategy for driving traffic to your site, and you will be unstoppable.

# Meet Bob

Because technical stuff can be hard to follow in the abstract, throughout this book we'll follow a fictional small businessman named Bob through his trials and tribulations in making over his website, which focuses on dogs and dog supplies. We'll track the development of his site from beginning to end. Bob is actually a composite of clients I've worked with over the past eleven years. Every question or situation Bob encounters is one I've dealt with before, under different circumstances. You can see the story of Bob, along with all of the examples shown here, by going to www.milliondollarwebsitebook.com.

Here's how Bob's story is presented in this book: After a concept is introduced and explained, the "Real Life" section will apply it to Bob's site. This way, you can see a practical version of the idea in action and how it might, hypothetically, affect Bob and his business.

## Bob's Story

Bob Smith, age thirty-seven, has always had a passion for dogs. Having been laid off from his job as an accountant at a start-up, he decides to take his savings and follow his real passion, and opens up a dog day-care center that also has a store that caters to all things dog.

He's got a great location in the hip area of town, and his store carries everything from dog toys to organic dog food to dog training tools. He's been selling a ton of what he's really famous for—his wife's Amazing HomeMade Biscuits. Even though there's a big chain pet store in the same town, discriminating customers go to Bob's because they love the environment and personal attention. His clientele is mostly twenty-five- to thirty-five-year-olds in the middle- to upper-income levels who treat their dogs like kids.

Many people have said that Bob's store is like a cool indie film or record store, only with dog stuff. They love that there's nothing cat- or bird-related in the store, that there's always cool music playing, and that Bob chooses smaller venders and healthier dog foods. Recently, he's become interested in eco-friendly pet supplies and food, and is becoming something of a source of this information in his town. If you want to know about how to be a "green dog owner," Bob's your man.

In short, Bob's Dogs is a booming small business. Bob works long hours, but he's happy and he loves the clientele.

After he'd been in business a while, several of his customers told him that he should really have a website, to give people information about the day care and boarding, as well as to sell the products.

*Great idea!* thought Bob. *I'll expand my business, possibly internationally. I'll be famous for my biscuits.*

At the very least, Bob figured he could use the website to spread the word about his store to neighboring communities and to provide street directions and hours to customers.

But here's the thing: Bob already worked overtime running his business, working in the store, and helping his wife bake the Amazing HomeMade Biscuits. Still, he did what many small business people do—he hired a designer friend to put together the website for his store, shown below. I think you'll agree, it has a lot going on.

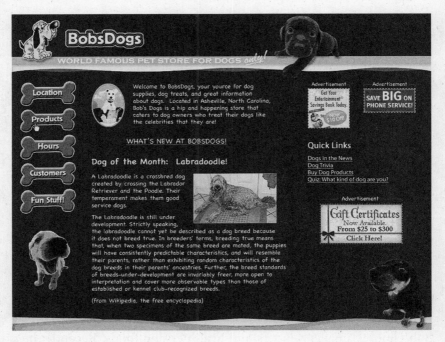

By Get Creative, Inc.

This site has been up for two years or so, isn't getting great traffic, and hasn't really made as many sales as Bob might want. Plus (and this is pretty important), after Bob's friend put up the site, he realized that it really wasn't that easy to make changes to it or to add sections (like the eco-friendly dog component, which he's just really gotten into in the past six months). About the only thing he's truly happy with is the storefront, which is actually hosted by another company (and launches when a user clicks "Products").

Note: Setting up the actual storefront and/or merchant account is beyond the scope of this book, but there are some great resources for this in Chapter 18. For now, I'm assuming that you (like Bob) have something up and running, and we're really just talking about the "front end" of the site—that is, how it looks and is organized.

In the future, Bob decides, he wants to have more control over the "back end," meaning that if he has a great idea or wants to add something, he can do that easily. Don't get me wrong—I'm not knocking Bob's designer friend. This site works fine just to have something up there, but in the long term, it needs some changes to make it better.

Remember, Bob owns a dog store because he loves dogs—not computers. He doesn't have time to read magazines on how to improve his traffic, to learn graphic design, and to teach himself about HTML and programs like Dreamweaver. Bob needs simple, straightforward tools for making his site the best it can be, without spending a lot of time and money on learning and implementing web-development and marketing strategies. Bob wants to sell dog stuff and make the world a better place, not sit in front of a computer all day. As for the long term, Bob has a list of stuff he eventually wants to do with the website. He knows the site needs to look different to reflect his brand and eco-consciousness, and he really wants to start using it more as a business tool and less as a brochure. He'd also like to capture email addresses, but isn't sure how to do it or what to do with them once he gets them. Plus, he has a great relationship with his local animal shelter and really wants to promote their site on his. But, like many small business owners, Bob is all ideas and no time. He has literally no idea where to start. Plus, he's been so frustrated in the past trying to make updates, he's gun-shy. So for the past year, Bob has been living with his head in the sand in terms of his website.

It's time for all that to change. Bob is going to take control of his website, and it's going to be less painful (and far more enjoyable) than he ever thought it could be. We'll follow along as Bob learns, step by step, how to make his website as awesome in real life as it is in his mind.

# REAL LIFE >>
## *How Bob Applies These Concepts to His Site*

AFTER I STOP Bob from hyperventilating about how much work he thinks this is going to be, I give him the basics of "what makes a good site" and talk to him a little about his target audience. Then I give Bob his first homework assignment: Look at your site with "fresh eyes" to determine its user-friendliness. He puts aside his fears, takes a long, hard look at his site, and decides that it's probably not as user-friendly as he originally thought. For example, he decides that if he were a customer, he would probably be annoyed that he had to go hunting around under "Products" to find the Amazing HomeMade Biscuits. He might also be frustrated at finding there is no clear "Contact Us" button reachable from the homepage, and that there's barely a mention of the day-care facility on the site, even though people tell him they go there just to find the hours and a map.

Bob realizes that his website is pretty messy-looking, too, and doesn't really reflect the clean and simple vibe that people get in his stores. Overall, the site doesn't get much traffic, orders are still pretty low, and Bob doesn't feel great about referring people there.

Bob then consults with a few of his most honest and Internet-savvy friends, asking for their no-holds-barred assessment of his site. These are the comments he receives:

"You can order stuff on this website?"
"I like the store better."
"I got lost in the site, got distracted, and decided to check my email."

At this point I meet with him, try to discern the overall goals and brand strategy of his store/site, and then analyze the site for usability, search engine optimization, content strategy, keyword density, and overall effectiveness in supporting his business. In the initial analysis of the site, I also point out glaring structural, architectural, and content errors that are holding him back. You can see the more immediate fixes in Chapter 7.

For now, my general assessment of Bob's website is as follows.

Bob's site is not immediately offensive to users—meaning, it doesn't have weird music, an obnoxious Flash intro, or any glaring technology errors. That said, neither the design nor the content are particularly engaging, and nothing on the site would entice someone to shop there rather than at a more widely recognized online store.

When I did a few searches for the site, using several standard search engines, nothing came up. Based on this, I'm pretty sure Bob hasn't submitted the site to search engines or put any keywords in his content, but it's still early, so I wouldn't expect him to have this knowledge yet. Still, from this analysis alone, I'm pretty sure no one is even finding his site.

Having visited the Bob's Dogs brick-and-mortar store and then checked out the site, it is evident that the website does not accurately reflect and do justice to Bob's company's brand. The site is much too generic to compete against corporate giants and is not niche market enough to capture a specialized online audience similar to that of his physical store.

At first glance, I would also note that Bob's site has:

- No links to other sites
- A minimal amount of relevant content
- No email capture mechanism
- Confusing categorization of information
- Slow loading speed
- A large amount of clutter

After thoroughly checking out the entire website, I'm still not sure what purpose it serves, other than to give me directions to the store. Of course, Bob has told me (in our meetings) that his objective in having a website is to drastically increase sales and to heavily promote his biscuits. Unfortunately, my professional opinion is that his site fails to create the kind of confidence and trust in users that would make them break away from their usual doggie fare at the big pet supply retailers, to try his unique biscuits and other specialty products, and to return to his site. Ultimately, if Bob is to compete with other online retailers, his site needs some work.

During our post-evaluation meeting, I lay all of this on the table for Bob—painful though it is (that's what I meant by tough love), along with a plan for upgrading his site. I enlist his help, asking him to think about and define his target audience and to describe his goals for the site. Also, while talking to Bob earlier, I realized that he is a dog expert and that he has a bunch of content in the form of pamphlets and brochures that he gives out in his store that could be utilized on the site. I encourage him to gather up all of this content, which will be really helpful in developing his site.

As Bob recovers from the shock of the initial analysis, let's move on to Chapter 2, where we will define your target audience, as well as gain an understanding of why this is important to know.

# 2 | Define Your Audience

When you know your users like the back of your hand, you can aim your site straight for the target and hit the bull's-eye time after time.

**Y**ou **don't have** to hire a big-name design firm and spend a million bucks to reap the benefits of using good tools to build your site. A website is simply an extension of your vision for your business, and like any successful component, it needs its own little business plan. This just means getting a few things straight before you touch a single thing on your site.

Defining who will be the primary and secondary users of your website can make a huge difference in the way you design your site, the technology you choose for it, and the content you put on it. Your primary users, or audience, are those for whom you're primarily making the site—that is, your target market, the people you hope will be using the site 90 to 95 percent of the time. Your secondary users would be anyone else you think might use the site.

This might seem obvious, but you'd be surprised how many people throw up a website without first profiling who their main users are, what those users' primary objectives are, and why and how their site can satisfy those objectives. If you're making a site to which you hope eighteen- to twenty-five-year-old guys will flock, it's going to look a lot different than, say, a site for new moms. Having a clear picture of who your users will be makes the job of designing a website much easier, since you'll be making your site for real people, not just an abstraction in your mind.

Whenever there's a question as to whether a design element—be it the colors, layout, words, images, or special features such as Flash—is appropriate for the site, you can just refer (and defer) to your primary and secondary user goals. If it doesn't match, don't bother. It's that simple.

For starters, let's check out two people with very different website profiles:

**User A.** An avid nature enthusiast, this guy loves to go on hikes and camping trips, and goes to websites that offer him deals on equipment as well as information about interesting places to travel. He doesn't want to see an advertisement for bath soap, anything pink, or any writing geared toward teenagers. He doesn't have high-speed access, so he doesn't like graphics that take too much time to load.

**User B.** This busy, conscientious young mom wants to order diapers online, not wade through fancy technology. She has to hold her baby with one hand while she surfs the Internet with the other. If you want her as a customer, your site should be easy to navigate, feature cute baby products, and give her a warm feeling. She has high-speed access, but doesn't have much time, so she wants just enough graphics to see what she's ordering.

Here's why stuff like this is important: Say your site for new moms, like User B, is doing very well and you're considering some new advertising prospects. Knowing your users the way you do, you would choose an ad for GapKids over an ad for an online casino, because you know your users are more likely to go to the Gap. Simple. Conversely speaking, you would not want that GapKids ad anywhere near a site you would make for User A. Why? Because User A would get fed up with flashy ads for a store he would never go to, and he would never come back.

\* \* \*

# Defining Your Who

To form a clear picture of who you want using your site, create a detailed profile of your ideal customers (your primary users, or audience). What do they look like? How old are they? What is their level of technical savvy? What are their income brackets, socioeconomic status, education levels, professions, personal interests, ethnicity, and cultures? How do they spend their time and their money? What are their favorite products within your business category? This ideal user is the person you should have in mind whenever you're designing, writing, or adding anything to the site.

So what's a secondary audience? This is anyone else who might use the site but that doesn't meet all the criteria of your primary user. While you want to make sure the content is still appropriate for them, the design, advertisements, and tone of your site are still mandated by the primary audience.

Don't get me wrong—I'm not saying you should try to please everyone. That will drive you nuts, and it never works. Just try to think of the *main* type of person who will use your site (your target demographic), and then think of a few possible secondary users, and you'll be fine.

Big companies don't even start making a website until they're 100 percent clear on who's going to use it. Here's an example: The site for SEGA games is clearly targeted toward young people (probably boys) who play video games. Take a look at www.sega.com. Flashy graphics, bold eye-catching colors, and content that features popular games are just a few of the ways SEGA is going to engage their target audience to become frequent visitors of their site (and frequent consumers of their games). Clever! SEGA definitely knows who their primary user is going to be, and has constructed its site accordingly.

As for the secondary users of the SEGA site, one might imagine that they'd be reporters, people looking for jobs, or other adult-types. For this small percentage, SEGA makes sure that these sections are easily located with small links like "Corporate" and "Careers," but I think you'll agree, this site is overwhelmingly targeted toward gamers.

Now let's take a look at a site with a completely different primary audience: BabyCenter.com. If possible, bring up BabyCenter's website in a different window and take a look at it right next to SEGA's site.

Wow, what a difference, right? BabyCenter is clearly targeted toward moms—moms to be, moms of toddlers, moms in general. Pastel colors and multiple images of cute babies tell us that this site is geared toward women (though I'm sure they wouldn't mind if some dads got in on the discussions too). Prominently displayed content elements include a pregnancy countdown clock (no doubt one of their most popular features), discussion forums (essential for moms of all stages), and articles about the most common challenges moms face, from getting pregnant to knowing the signs of labor to potty training your toddler and beyond. BabyCenter is well organized, so anyone else who's using this site, maybe to get information about employment or research an article, can easily find what he or she is looking for. This is all achieved without once losing site of the target audience.

By thinking of who is going to use the site 95 percent of the time and then giving a little thought to the other 5 percent, you too can put together a great site that serves all of your purposes. This information and awareness will allow you to construct user scenarios—that is, stories about who your users are and what they might do on your site.

I know what you're thinking: Writing fictional bios of customers you don't even have yet seems like a weird thing to do. Believe me, I felt like an idiot the first time I sat in my office writing, "Jenny is twenty-five years old and works at a cosmetics company," but I quickly realized the value of this exercise when it came time to design the site. Over the years, writing user scenarios has helped me create some of the best-known websites out there.

Just to get you started in defining your ideal customer, below are some snippets from actual user scenarios that I've written for big companies over the years.

## Mary, Age 23
### *Sales manager (office job)/high-speed Internet connection*

Web-savvy, but doesn't like a lot of frills. Using the Internet is second nature to her; she's been at it since high school. She is totally intolerant of bad technology, such as shopping carts that don't work, too much Flash, and similar problems. She is more likely than someone with less online experience to take a risk on a small company, but she is also more likely to get upset if something goes wrong. She values professionalism and good content, and often spends time reading articles and educating herself about products before buying.

## Rick, Age 35
### *Personal trainer/high-speed Internet connection*

Somewhat web-savvy. Goes online daily to check email, uses MapQuest, and buys things online at big sites like Amazon.com. Uses Google to search. Does not spend a lot of time online, so he wants the sites he does use to be efficient and not waste his time. Is impressed by good design.

## Andy, Age 19
### *College student/high-speed wireless connection*

On the "bleeding edge" of being tech savvy—that is, he knows way more about technology than most web developers. Is an avid online gamer, playing for several hours each day with others in his dorm. To impress him, your site must be heavy on the flashy technology, otherwise he's bored.

Do any of these people sound like the primary audience for your website? If so, take them, expand upon them, and use them when you're developing or reworking your site. What's most important is that you have a picture of a real person in your head when you're making decisions about your site.

When you're constructing similar stories about your primary and secondary audiences, just think about the people you know and how they use the Internet. Your dad probably wants different things from a website than you would, and you probably want different things than your neighbor. The clearer you can make the picture in your mind of who your users are and what they want, the better you can tailor your site to people who fit that profile. In other words, the better you know your user, the more successful your site will be. Period. In general business lingo, this is known as defining your target audience (your market demographic).

Creating these mini-profiles of your ideal customer and your next-best customer might seem like a lot of work in the beginning, but it really helps in developing a long-term strategy for your site. From now on, for every design element and for every piece of content you want to put on your site, you will first take into consideration your primary user's point of view.

For example, your site sells designer handbags, and Mary is your primary user. She gets your newsletter, has bought several things from your site, and recommends you to her friends. One day, you decide that you're going to expand your site by putting up some banner ads. You'll want to make sure that the ads have Mary as their primary audience, too—that means no ads for sports, cars, men's deodorant, and so forth—or you're likely to make Mary think that (a) you don't know her at all, and (b) you're selling her out.

Remember: Content that doesn't serve your primary audience serves no purpose. In fact, it can create a cross-purpose, making your site seem like it's off-strategy and confusing your users, maybe even driving some of them away. People like to frequent sites that clearly have them in mind—that old birds-of-a-feather quality. When they're on a site, they are there for a specific and often single purpose, and like to think about only one thing at a time. So if you stick an ad for a mortgage broker on your site, in the time it takes Mary to shift gears from handbags to mortgages, she might have lost a little faith in you.

Each feature and function of your website—even the smallest sliver of content, like a one-line ad—must be relevant to and of interest to your primary audience. Stick with this one rule, and you will be ahead of 90 percent of your competition.

## Defining Your What

Now that you have decided who will be using your site, it's time to decide what you want them to do there. Would you like them to complete a transaction? What will they need and want to know about you, your business, your site, and your products? This is where your information architecture comes into play, because what you want your primary user to do on your site will determine not only what you put on your site but also how you organize it.

The first time Mary comes to your site, you want her to like it. You want her to enter her email address to sign up for your mailing list. You want her to spend some time reading your content, looking at your products, and hopefully, completing a transaction. In short, you want to engage Mary so that she converts as quickly as possible from user to customer. The better you know Mary and what you want her to do, the more focused you can make the content of the site.

Let's look at an example that illustrates both a well-focused who and what . . . Log on to Mattel's Barbie website at www.barbie.com.

Can you tell the primary audience for this site? The objective? (These are not trick questions.)

Clearly, the site's target audience is little girls who love Barbie dolls. From the cool animated graphics to the primarily pink color scheme and trendy girly catchphrases, this site is designed to appeal to little girls who are crazy for Barbie. The look and feel of the site and its specific features and content are geared toward these primary users, with the objective of making them want to hang out on the site, watch the videos, do the activities, and get even more into Barbie. Mattel (the maker of Barbie) could have gone in a number of directions with Barbie.com. They could have used the site simply to promote the doll to kids without providing any fun stuff for them to do on the site. They could have chosen to target parents who might buy the products for their kids. Or they could have forgone the branding opportunity and just redirected users to Mattel's corporate site (which is probably geared more toward wholesalers and retailers than to consumers). They did none of these things. Instead, they chose to target little girls who love Barbie. And the objective of this site is equally clear: to create a world for little girls who love Barbie.

If we look a little closer at this site, we'll see that it's not all that easy to buy a Barbie doll from this world, because little girls who hang out in a virtual Barbie world are not going to buy a Barbie doll online. Sure, there is a "Shop with Barbie" link, but its primary objective is to get kids to create a "wishlist." If they actually want to buy something, they are directed off the site, and given a clear warning to check with their parents.

This two-tiered system is very effective. Kids can hang out on the site and create the wishlist, and then turn to their parents for the actual purchase. Essentially, Barbie.com just creates the desire for the products, then lets the sale take care of itself, elsewhere. Again, very clever!

While we're speaking of parents, kids, and toys, let's compare Barbie.com to the website for Toys "R" Us (www.toysrus.com).

This site, while being vaguely kid-friendly and obviously loaded with merchandise for kids, has a totally different target audience: parents of kids who want toys, and it is a lean, mean, toy-selling machine. The people who designed this site know that parents are busy, need minimal incentive between impulse and purchase, and have zero time for frilly add-ons. Thus, there are no special kiddie activities and content here.

Instead, this site includes features that adult online Toys "R" Us shoppers are apt to appreciate most: clean navigation, a constantly visible shopping cart, concise purchasing instructions, and the Toys "R" Us logo with a page marker prominently displayed so the users always know exactly where they are on the site. Toysrus.com also has a smart architecture, with well-marked sections for sales, hot items, boys, girls, and different age groups. So when parents select "Birth to 12 Months," for example, they can be reasonably sure they are not going to be confronted with a mountain bike, clothes for a seven-year-old, video games, or toys that are inappropriate for a baby. This site makes it easy for users to find and make their selection, and then get on with the business of becoming a customer.

## Defining Your Why

Okay, you've decided who's going to your site and what you want them to do there. And that leads naturally to the next key question: Why would they do this? The more thoroughly you've defined the site's who and what, the easier it will be to define (and create) the why.

In other words: Why would your primary users choose your site over another site—or, for that matter, an off-line competitor? Have you chosen a design style and tone as well as colors, images, and language that fit your target audience? Do you have engaging content that lets them know you "get" them and want them to be your customers forever? Is it organized in a way that will appeal and make sense to them? Are the features and technology appropriate for those "whos"?

To illustrate the importance of the why, let's look at Apple's website (www.apple.com). Go ahead, go there now. They change their site all the time, so they've probably got something you haven't seen.

Now . . . ask yourself this: Why would you buy a computer from the Apple website rather than at a discount store? You know that you can probably get a deal from one of those dime-a-dozen MacTropolis kind of places, right? So what would compel you to buy the computer at Apple.com?

The answer to this question is the elusive "why." Simply put, you buy the computer from this site or at the Apple store because Apple makes you feel like you're a part of something—a community of like-minded Apple devotees, all of whom value progressive design, a good website, and the "world" that is created by Apple Computer on this site. Apple knows its audience, expertly markets to them, and makes it worth the price of admission to repeatedly make purchases from them. Why would you go anywhere else? You've got everything you need right on this site, including the feeling that you're part of something bigger than yourself.

The overall "Apple feeling" starts the minute you hit the homepage, where you'll always find super high-quality photos or graphics of the beautifully designed Apple products. Whether or not you're actually a Mac person, you have to agree that Apple's strength is design, and this is evident both on the website and in the products that have made them famous. Apple's homepage photography usually highlights a cool new product, showing it in such wonderful graphic detail that you might just have to buy one right then, which you can do just by visiting the Apple Store on the site. If you need support for an existing Apple product, they're there for you. If you need to download something, it's also right there. They also have a whole section just for iTunes, which has proven to be a hugely successful delivery system for music. Additionally, Apple is always coming up with new products to help you better organize your life, and they've put those in their own section as well.

Overall, despite having such a huge amount of information to deliver, Apple still makes the architecture of its site amazingly simple. Staying on this site (or visiting an Apple store) for any length of time might just convert you into a Mac person. It happened to me!

## Defining Your How

How will your primary users navigate your site, access your content, and complete a transaction? Just as you created a scenario in order to picture who your primary users are, to determine how they use your site, you trace the path they would take through your site, as though creating a mental video in which you are clicking and seeing through their eyes.

For example, let's take a look at the site I work on for Johnson & Johnson, DiscoverNursing.com (shown below). The primary audience for this site is students or potential students interested in finding out more about the nursing profession. Secondary audience members include nurses and press.

By Johnson & Johnson Services, Inc.

One possible path for one of these primary users (the students) might be:

1. Arrive at the homepage, look around.
2. Click the "View Nursing Benefits & Salaries" link, which takes the visitor to the "Why > Benefits & Salaries" section for more information on salaries for nurses and the benefits available to nurses. (We're assuming this person knows nothing about the nursing profession, so this is a good place to start.)
3. Visit the "What > Nursing: The Basics" section for more information on how, specifically, one becomes a nurse.
4. Visit the "What > Nursing Careers" section for information on hundreds of different nursing specialties.
5. Visit the "Who > Profiles" section to read stories about real nurses and their paths to success.
6. Visit the "How > Program Search" database to find programs in the user's area.
7. Click through to one of the universities returned by the search, and hopefully get more information.
8. Visit the "How > Scholarship Search" database to find scholarships that might help pay for nursing school.

By constructing pathways for primary users through your site, you will prepare yourself to make better decisions when it comes to everything from information architecture to what to put on the homepage. This exercise helps you keep your primary user in mind when you're organizing the content and writing for the site. Before you touch anything, you must ask yourself "Would Mary get this? Would this be something she would be able to find, or would she care about this?" If the answer is no to any of these, then chances are it doesn't belong on your site. Bottom line: Always keep the user in mind!

\* \* \*

# Practice Makes Perfect

Take a look at the following websites, each of which has a different target audience:

**MTV:** www.mtv.com

**BMW:** www.bmw.com

**Home Depot:** www.homedepot.com

**Amazon:** www.amazon.com

After looking around a little bit, try to determine the following:

▶ **What is the primary audience for the site?** Can you tell just by look-ing? Clearly, the MTV site is for a completely different target audience than the BMW site. Keep this in mind when designing (or redesigning) your site. For example, if your site is about spas, resorts, and international travel for middle-aged women, you probably don't want to use a bunch of animated Flash graph-ics better suited to the teenage video-gamers of MTV. Similarly, HomeDepot.com's customers probably just want to get in, find the product they need or a store near them, and get out without a lot of flashy stuff and hassle. Just a guess, but I'm assuming Home Depot is never going to redesign their site with pastel col-ors, because this just wouldn't work for their target audience.

Use this exercise to start yourself thinking about your primary users and what they might like (and not like). Let familiarity with your customers, as well as plain old common sense, be your guide in selecting the content, architecture, technology, style, and tone of your site. The more specific you can make your user scenarios, the higher will be the number of first-time visitors who become your actual customers (your conversion rate). If you're stumped by this list of design elements, not to worry—we'll be covering them (that is, what generally works for which target audience) in Chapter 10. This exercise is just to get you thinking in terms of *your* target audience, and what in general might and might not appeal to them.

▶ **What is the objective of the site?** Just by looking at the homepage, can you tell what you're supposed to do/learn/gather from this website? Are they trying to sell you socks? Building up your interest in their brand/products? Trying to get you to join their mailing list for updates?

▶ **What do they want you to do?** Good websites show *and* tell the user what to do, with engaging graphics and compelling content. If you leave users dangling or wandering around aimlessly, or give them too many choices, they are likely to go somewhere else, probably to a site that is more focused and more clearly "for" them.

▶ **Can I easily find the information I'm looking for?** Nothing drives an eager user away faster than wanting something specific and having to search deep within your site to find it. Amazingly, it is often the simplest piece of information—such as the "Contact Us" button or the shopping cart—that is the most difficult to find on poorly designed sites. Don't trust that the user is going to look very hard for anything. If it's not easy to find, it might as well not even be there.

▶ **Can I easily figure out how to complete a transaction?** For instance, Amazon.com wants you to buy books, CDs, DVDs, and a wide range of other products, and they have the item search, selection, and ordering process down to a science. They make it easy to find stuff; they put a big "Buy It" button right by the thing you were looking for; and they've made the checkout process almost effortless. You can go to Amazon with a book in mind, find it, buy it, and check out in less than five minutes. This is what makes Amazon one of the top online retailers in the world.

# REAL LIFE >>
## *Bob Defines His Audience*

BOB HAS A very good picture of his ideal user, since many of his customers are friends and former coworkers who love their dogs more than life itself. He estimates his primary customers range in age from twenty-five to thirty-five years old and that (according to his records) they spend a lot of their disposable incomes on dogs and dog products.

He's noticed that most of his customers are women and gay men, with the occasional husband or boyfriend in tow. After some brief resistance ("Is this really necessary?"), he constructs the following user scenario, based on how he'd like the site to perform when his ideal user comes a-callin':

## Susan, Age 32
*Very Internet savvy, but doesn't like a lot of frills or fancy technology*

**Who.** She has completed many purchases online, and she feels comfortable navigating around websites. Susan has a low tolerance for things like broken links and typos, as she feels it makes sites look unprofessional. She is inclined to give new sites and recommendations from friends a chance.

**What.** Susan is inclined to spend large amounts of money on her dog, who is her surrogate child. She hears about Bob's Amazing Biscuits from a friend, and checks out the site. Ideally, Bob would like Susan to become a regular customer, buying at least one bag of dog food per month, along with as many Amazing HomeMade Biscuits as her dogs can eat. Bob wants Susan to come to the site, love it, complete a transaction, and keep returning for many years to come.

**Why.** Bob wants his site to engage Susan on a level that the big retailers just can't—with great customer service, articles that are specific to her needs, and an overall "vibe" that matches his bricks-and-mortar store, where Susan is a regular. Susan wants to support Bob's business and often drives over to the store to buy stuff, but so far hasn't gotten into the website because it looks a little unprofessional and she can't find anything. Bob wants her to hang out there, talk to other dog owners in a forum, and of course, regularly order the dog biscuits. He plans to do this with the same seamless shopping experience that she's come to expect from a big corporate site. Although Bob's Dogs is a small business, he can offer the personalized service and the real-life canine knowledge that a big retailer cannot, while still being just as professional as they are.

**How.** Susan should be able to find things easily on Bob's site, the content should engage her, and she should "get it" it right away. Her first impression of the site should be that it's well organized, she can easily find what she's looking for, she's interested in many of the articles on the site, and the site offers at least one item (gourmet biscuits) that she can't find elsewhere. She should sign up for the mailing list, complete a transaction, and bookmark the page for return visits. This means Bob is going to have to change the organization of his site so that at first glance, it's much easier for Susan to find things like articles. He's also going to have to add the "Forum" feature so that Susan can connect with other dog owners, and put the good articles he's been sitting on in their own section, so that users like Susan can find them. Finally, he's going to really highlight those biscuits, so that with one click, Susan can easily satisfy her dog's cravings. Overall, Bob's going to need to make his site much better organized and easy to navigate, so that Susan wants to hang out there, and to come back.

To continue with the excellent experience, when Susan does make a purchase on Bob's website, she should immediately receive a receipt of her purchase in a well-written, clear email. She should also receive a confirmation email when she signs up for the mailing list. Her order should arrive on time and should include exactly the items she ordered. If she has any questions, the website should feature either a "Contact" button or an email address that gets her directly to a customer service person or Bob himself, and the packing slip should include a toll-free telephone number so that she can talk to a real person if she needs to.

In short, although Bob is running a small business (and a small business website), it needs to function as smoothly as a big business in order to build Susan's confidence and keep her coming back. Bob's site (like any good website), should be well organized, appropriate to his target audience, and have large amounts of good content as well as things to buy. Like any good site, Bob's site should never leave users feeling lost, or confused, or make them think that Bob doesn't really have a handle on what he's doing. Really, the best websites are easy, and focused, and almost transparent to users, who shouldn't have to bother themselves finding where things are or think about why things are misspelled.

Each of these elements plays an integral role in a professional website, and not all of them always happen on Bob's site now. We're going to change all that, though, and make Bob's site everything he's always hoped it could be.

So where is your site in the "Who, What, Why, and How?" Do you have a clear picture of who's coming to your site, why, what you want them to do when they get there, and how you want them to do it? I guarantee you—if you don't know, neither will your user. Getting clear on your primary users (and what you want them to do) now is the first step in the construction (or reconstruction) of your website. Make sure this step is done right before you proceed. Even taking a few minutes to make some notes about your primary user can make a world of difference in your overall site.

# 3 | Make Your Keyword List

Creating a killer keyword list will snag users far and wide and drive them straight to your site.

**O**nce you've got a handle on who you want coming to your site, the next step is to figure out what search words they're using to get there, so you can use those words in the site's construction. These "keywords" make the difference between a good site, and a good site with tons of traffic.

Like many of the topics in this book, the subject of keywords is one on which an entire book can be (and has been) written. Given the tools in this chapter, you can spend as much or as little time on the subject of keywords as you choose. Keyword research can be fun (and somewhat addictive), and it's an endeavor that some people have based entire companies on. But, since you probably want to know what keywords have to do with your site, where to find them, and what to do with them, let's get to it! If, after reading this chapter, you end up opening your own keyword research company, more power to you.

Of all the mistakes I see people making with websites, not having a decent keyword list is, by far, the most frequent and most harmful. Taking the time to properly build a keyword list will make a world of difference in attracting users—and a higher percentage of users with the potential to convert to customers—to your website.

Keywords are just that—the words that users type into search engines to find what they're looking for. From the site owner's point of view, keywords are those commonly known terms and phrases that describe the nature of your business and your products. For example, a website for an online tea shop might include the keywords "specialty teas," "gourmet tea," "teapots," "teacups," "cozies," and "gift baskets."

From a web consultant's point of view, keywords are what we use to do search engine optimization—otherwise known as kicking competitors' asses in the keyword search arena. Professional website developers use keywords to:

▸ Analyze market need and profit potential of websites.
▸ Embed the site's content with a sufficient supply of in-demand keywords.
▸ Maximize pay-per-click advertising opportunities (as on Google or Yahoo!, see Chapter 17).
▸ Enrich meta tags, alt tags, and other strategic places on the website, should you choose to do so (outlined in Chapter 15).

If you're still not convinced, take the word of Mike Mindel, whose company, Wordtracker, has become a million dollar business by offering keyword research from real search results: "Keywords are simply the words people use when they search. Incorporate those words into your website copy and your position in search engines' results will rise—often dramatically—and that means more sales online," says Mike.

So what does all this mean to you? Think of keywords in terms of the standard supply-and-demand economic theory. Words people use to search for things on the Internet are the demand. Websites that contain these sought-after words are the supply. When you integrate into your website keywords that users demand, you become, via search engines, an identifiable source of supply. The smarter you are at supplying the right keywords on your site, the more in demand your site will be.

# Where in the World Wide Web Are Keywords?

This is one of those "this info might be worth the whole price of the book" moments. If you know where to look, the Internet has a wealth of free information out there that will help you identify and research the best keywords for your site. Not only do these tools tell you how many users search the Internet for these words, they also provide the user search stats for keywords similar to yours, including some you probably hadn't thought of. If any of those similar terms apply to your business, make sure to add them to your keyword list.

## Google AdWords Keyword Tool
*https://adwords.google.com/select/KeywordToolExternal*

We'll get to what the different Google AdWords programs are and how to use them in Chapters 12 and 17, but for now please take advantage of the completely free research tool that Google provides. All you need to do to get a feel for how many people are searching for what you're selling is go to this nifty tool and type in a keyword (like "dog food," or "bibs," or "spa vacations," or whatever your site is mostly focused on). From there, the Keyword Tool will tell you how many people searched for that word in the previous month, as well as providing you with a totally handy list of similar words and their search rates. You're going to want to scroll all the way down to the bottom and export the list for Excel.

. For now, don't sign up for an ad campaign. Just focus on building the keyword list. Just doing this exercise opens exciting new doors. There are tons of people out there searching for what you're selling, plus they're searching for related things you didn't even think of. This will give you all sorts of ideas. Just FYI, the Google AdWords Keyword Tool is only telling you how many Google searches are being performed, and does not take into account any of the remaining search engines, such as Yahoo!, Ask.com, MSN, or others.

## Wordtracker's Free Keyword Suggestion Tool
*http://freekeywords.wordtracker.com/*

Wordtracker is a London-based company that offers extensive keyword research for search engine marketers and website owners. This free tool can help you add to the list you started with Google Adwords and further help you build your site. Wordtracker's results are compiled from several different search engine "crawlers," specifically Dogpile and Metacrawler, and they claim to have a database of 330 million terms whose search frequency they continually update. If you end up absolutely loving keyword research and want to delve deeper, by all means take the Wordtracker seven-day free trial. After that, monthly subscriptions start in the $59 range. For now, though, try out the tool and use it to add to your list, give you new ideas, and get you further excited about how many people are buying what you're selling.

## Building Your Keyword List

In order to make your website successful, you must make sure that the words *on your site* and the words *for which people are searching* are the same. If your site is not keyword rich (meaning it has the right supply of in-demand keywords), the search engines will be unlikely to find it.

Your assignment, should you choose to accept it, is to use the tools I've introduced above to build a keyword list—right now, before you start creating (or revamping) your website—which you will use later to design a site that search engines are sure to find, sending a slew of new users your way. Having a killer keyword list will help you create great content for your site (Chapter 9), raise your search engine ranking (Chapters 14 and 15), and create an effective pay-per-click advertising campaign to drive more traffic to your site (Chapter 17). Frankly, I can see no downside to doing this research.

This exercise requires a few minutes, an Excel spreadsheet, and a keen sense of curiosity. With these three things, you can home in on which keywords are most likely to drive users to your site and pretty much estimate how many of them are interested in buying what you're selling.

Building your keyword list will involve the following steps:

1. Create an Excel spreadsheet named Keyword Research. You will be adding to this spreadsheet after the initial research, if you expand your inventory or get more ambitious with your online advertising.

2. Go to the Google AdWords Keyword Tool (https://adwords .google.com/select/KeywordToolExternal) and start by typing in the most general word or words that relate to your site. In Bob's case, these would be the words "dog food."

3. Copy and paste the list generated by the Keyword Tool into your spreadsheet for future reference. Right now, you're just trying to generate a list of search words/terms that might lead people to your site. Copy and paste all the words that come up, even if they only had a hundred searches last month. Later, when we cover online advertising, I'll show you how to use those infrequently searched keywords to your advantage.

4. Keep typing in words—you'll find some crazy stuff that will rapidly build up your keyword list. This exercise is fun!

5. Repeat with Wordtracker's free tool (http://freekeywords .wordtracker.com). Keep going until you have at least 250 words. (This will not be difficult.) Wordtracker's tool will give you 100 words at a time.

Once you've built your keyword list, you can (and should) keep adding to it, as you think of other keywords that apply to your business, build your website, expand your product line, and add content to your site. In the process of building and updating your keyword list, you will probably also stumble across and brainstorm other ideas for your site, so always keep a notebook handy to jot them down.

# REAL LIFE >>
## *Bob Builds His Keyword List*

BOB WAS UNFAMILIAR with the concept of keywords and didn't use any to build his site originally. He is enthusiastic about being able to see what people are actually searching for on the Internet. He starts by typing the words "dog food" into the Google Adwords Keyword Tool and is blown away to see there were more than 100,000 searches for that term last month. Upon further searching, Bob discovers that there are many people searching for what he sells: 21,416 searches for "dog treats," 4,000 for "homemade dog biscuits," and even 1,300 for the term "gourmet dog biscuit." He does the same thing with the eco-friendly theme and gets a ton of keywords and ideas from those searches as well. Now that he knows what people want, his creative juices are flowing; he knows he can supply what they are demanding.

Clearly, there is an audience for what Bob is selling; he just has to target his niche, make his site better, and his sales will go up.

Using the keyword research tools, Bob easily builds a list of almost a thousand keywords, which he puts into an Excel spreadsheet for safekeeping and future use. Bob also gets a few great ideas from some of the crazy searches he turns up—everything from "vegan dog food" to "toys for small dogs" and "designer dog biscuits." The exercise convinces him that he can supply what the people searching for these items want. Now, it's just a matter of letting them know he's out there.

Like Bob, you'll want to use these keyword research tools to build up an arsenal of words and phrases that will help you with everything from content creation to website organization (because you'll know what people are searching for the most). Keyword research will help you with advertising and with new ideas for your business and your site, and (should you want to get really fancy) keywords can even be inserted right into your site's code to make the site even more magnetic to search engines. Once you've got the keyword list nailed down, you're already ahead of 90 percent of your small business competition—and it's only Chapter 3!

Next up, we'll find out some things about how your site is working now, always with an eye toward improvement.

# Research and Discovery

**A**fter you've defined your primary audience and nailed down your keywords, it's helpful to collect every piece of information that might aid you in knowing which direction the site needs to go. After all, if you don't know where you are, you can't tell where you want to go.

During this research and discovery process, you will do several things, including:

- Solicit opinions about your current site (or conduct tests)
- Identify five sites that you like
- Determine what you like about them
- Find and analyze your traffic statistics
- Calculate your site's conversion rate
- Identify any best sellers (among your products/services) that should be featured
- Review user suggestions, questions, and comments

Notice that none of these steps include actually changing anything on your site yet. This research phase is where you will do the legwork of developing your content strategy. Without it, your site will merely be another in a galaxy of websites that gets larger every day. Don't fall into the trap of wanting to just throw something up there. Execution without strategy is only going to hurt you in the long run.

Don't worry, many parts of the research and discovery phase are actually fun, and it will give you some great ideas for where you want your site to go.

# 4 Borrow from the Best

Explore successful sites and discover how to apply their winning web strategies to your site.

**T**he first part of your research and discovery mission is actually pretty simple, as it involves visiting sites that you go to every day (or at least regularly). It's time to do some website exploration, which I am certain will lead you to some enlightening discoveries. First, we'll check out a few of what I consider to be the best sites on the web, and then you'll visit a few of your top picks. After taking a closer look at these sites (and with a little assistance from yours truly), you'll learn how to use some of the best features of the best sites out there on your own site.

Among the surprising discoveries that I suspect you will make during this exploratory process is the realization that you already know a great deal more about usability, information architecture, and good web design than you think you do. By now, you've no doubt visited and used numerous websites in both your personal and professional life, and you probably have a good idea of what you like and dislike about them.

When you're thinking analytically about your site—whether because you're building it for the first time, making some adjustments, or planning a redesign—it's really helpful to look at a few sites that you like while thinking about the concept of usability. Think of yourself as a cyber-detective who is trying to sleuth out the content strategy and the user interface design of each top-notch site. Once you've identified what makes a site tops in your book, you can then take that knowledge and apply similar elements to your site.

First, let's visit a website that tracks the "Top Online Retailers by Conversion Rate." This list comes out every month, and it's always very interesting to see who's on the list, what they have in common, and what new strategies they're trying out. I would recommend looking at this list every month—just by doing this, you will start to notice some very interesting trends in website development, such as "many of these sites are using pictures of real people," or "green seems to be a hot new color." Whether or not you change your site to reflect what's working for the top online retailers, it is always helpful to know what the big boys are doing, and what they're getting right.

You can see these top retailers (and what their conversion rates were) by visiting the "Conversion Rates" section of the informative GrokDotCom blog of a marketing company called FutureNow, which you can find at www.grokdotcom.com/category/conversion-rates.

Better yet, sign up for their free mailing list, and they'll send you website marketing tips as well as the monthly "Top Online Retailers" report. Spend a few minutes clicking through to each one, and try to get a feel for what they're doing, just for informational purposes. The more aware you are of what the really successful sites are doing, the more ideas you will have when it comes to your own site.

Now that you've seen who the leaders are (and hopefully identified a few things that they're doing well), let's do an exercise I like to call My Top Five Sites. I do this with all my new clients, sometimes at the first meeting, and it always turns out to be an amazingly insightful and beneficial exercise.

## My Top Five Sites

These sites made it into my Top Five list because they function smoothly, are well laid out, and provide a superior user experience. While you're looking at them, feel free to write down any other sites that come to mind or that you use frequently. Once you've gotten my take on some of my favorite sites, you can go to your top sites and review them with a sharper eye.

## Apple
*www.apple.com*

Always among my Top Five. Beautiful graphics integrated with catchy writing, clear instructions on what to do, and good information architecture. It's tough to get lost on this site, even though it features literally thousands of pages. Not only is the website well organized, it also has a similar feeling to being in an Apple store. Both the site and the stores are distinctively "Apple"—and immediately recognizable as such. This is called brand consistency—when both the image and message that a company projects are consistent throughout their products, stores, printed marketing materials, media presence, and website. Apple is an excellent model of brand consistency across their website, all of their marketing media, and their physical stores.

Too few businesses follow Apple's shining example of consistent and distinctive branding, particularly with their websites. In my consulting business, I have noticed that companies almost across the board will choose a generic look for their website, rather than making it look and feel like the company brand. This is a huge missed opportunity. For example, all of the elements of your website design—the color scheme, logo, tone of the writing, layout, type of imagery used, marketing message (or theme), and so on—should be compatible with any marketing materials (such as brochures and TV commercials) or online advertisements that reference or lead to your website. Otherwise, at least some of your users will think they've typed in the wrong URL and immediately leave.

That does not mean that your website should be an exact replica of, say, your brochure or that it should include the exact same verbiage as, say, your radio commercial. The Internet is a unique medium that calls for some design variety. But the visual image and the marketing message you present should be consistent—and immediately recognizable to your audience—in whatever medium you present it: brochures, press releases, TV and radio commercials, store signage, website, whatever. That might mean that all of your branding media (including your website) have the same color scheme, or the same logo and tagline (such as Nike's "Just Do It."), or the same overall tone. If your brochures and advertisements have an edgy tone and a young, hip, urban theme, for example, make sure that this tone and this theme carry through to your website.

Sometimes, you can correct minor inconsistencies between your web design and your other branding media by simply eyeballing and tweaking a few things to help give everything the same look, feel, message, tone, and so on. That may require hiring the same design professional to do (or redo) everything. Whatever it takes, do it and you'll be way ahead of the game.

## Baby.com: The Johnson & Johnson Family of Companies
*www.baby.com*

Speaking of brand consistency, I'd be hard-pressed to find a site that does it better than one of my other favorites, Baby.com, produced by Johnson & Johnson. This site brings together many of the Johnson & Johnson companies that offer baby products. Johnson & Johnson has built a reputation for being among the most trusted companies in the United States. One of the ways they have achieved this distinction is by building a strong brand focused on the nurturing bond between mother and child, and carrying this focus consistently across every type of communication Johnson & Johnson produces, from television ads to annual reports, brochures, and websites.

Baby.com is no exception and echoes that distinctive (and highly successful) Johnson & Johnson brand. The site is also well organized, clean, and engaging. The feel-good design invites you to come in, read through their library of thousands of articles by subject matter experts, and confidently purchase products from a brand you trust. The user experience at Baby.com is so positive that it encourages customers to keep coming back for all their baby needs.

\* \* \*

## Daily Candy
*www.dailycandy.com*

This is probably the best "know your demographic" example I can think of; almost every woman I know either knows about this site or gets their daily emails, and of their huge subscriber base, 95 percent are female, with an average age of thirty-one. There are many things to like about this site—its design is great, it's simple, and the editorial staff does an amazing job of culling through countless submissions to provide you with the best stuff that's happening in your town that day. Daily Candy has been hugely successful because they've stuck to their purpose—to provide the newest and latest info about beauty, fashion, and any other hip thing that's happening in your city. Originally founded by journalist Dany Levy as "a new, immediate way to share information while it was still fresh and actionable, with an affluent, influential female audience," this up-to-the-moment guide now has a presence in thirteen cities, including New York, San Francisco, Los Angeles, and London.

How successful are they? Well, from 2003 to 2008 they grew from 200,000 subscribers to over 2.5 million, and in August of 2008, they were bought by Comcast for $125 million. I have no doubt they'll be providing fashion and beauty news for years to come.

## Craigslist
*www.craigslist.com*

Founded in 1995 as a way for a guy named Craig to send out event announcements, Craigslist has become a phenomenon of growth and community interaction. Over the course of this book, you'll find that I love recommending Craigslist; not only do I think it's a feat of simplicity and great information architecture, but I am constantly amazed by how that site manages to connect people at all levels and with all sorts of needs. Craigslist is empowering because it brings people together—it's that simple. With new cities (and now countries) being added very frequently, this site is proof that you don't need fancy graphics to make your site succeed. In fact, after all these years—even after all of the attention and expansion this site has had—Craigslist still uses the same, plain text format and simple design, and it's one of the most successful sites out there.

## Target
### *www.target.com*

Ah, if only all of Target's physical stores could be as clean and well functioning as their website. As my friend Steve, the former VP of a major media outlet that includes five international websites, says, "Target's website has just enough Flash technology to impress without being overpowering. They also make great use of white space."

Target.com is intuitively laid out, so that you can make a decision about where you want to go next based solely on a quick glance at the homepage. Plus, their overall design is consistent throughout the site, even though they carry a wide variety of products, ranging from books to screwdrivers to Isaac Mizrahi handbags.

# The Power of Simplicity

As you can see, all of my Top Five Sites have several things in common. They are all very user-friendly and have excellent, easy-to-use functionality. Each site has a clear design and interesting content. And they all convey a brand image and brand message that is distinctive and consistent with their entire enterprise.

My favorite sites also have one other important thing in common: The designs are all simple. Why is simplicity important? In this age of "many pieces of information per second," I am always grateful to website designers who care enough to cut through the chaos of the Internet to provide users with a simple, elegant experience. Combine a simple design with interesting information, well-written content, and high-quality images, and you've got yourself a winner.

Now, you try!

With the new knowledge you've gained from looking over my favorite sites, you can now make a list of your Top Five Sites and evaluate them with a critic's eye. As I said before, you probably already know more about what makes for good web design than you realize.

Most people, certainly those actively involved in a business, use the Internet on a daily basis, and in the process they have developed opinions about the things they like and don't like about their favorite (and least favorite) sites. Why not put this firsthand experience and practical knowledge to use in improving your own website?

One of the easiest and most effective ways to create an optimum user experience on your site is to borrow the high points and avoid the mistakes of sites *you actually use*. If you've never really paid attention to this before (though most people do, if only at a subconscious level), now is a good time to start. Being able to pinpoint what *you* think is a positive feature or a negative feature of a website will come in handy when you're trying to put yourself in your users' shoes in designing a site on their behalf.

Just as I always ask new clients to name and critique their five favorite websites, as your satellite website consultant, I am now asking you to do the same. You might want to grab a pen and paper to write down your observations as you review your favorite websites. Here are a few questions to start with:

1. Which sites do you visit on a regular basis?
2. Which are your five favorite sites?
3. What do you like about each of these sites?
4. What do you dislike about each of these sites?

Here are a few other things to think about as you evaluate each site:

▶ What is this site about?
▶ What do they want me to do?
▶ How easy is it for me to accomplish this?
▶ Who is the target audience of this site?
▶ How do the design, color, and writing reflect awareness of this audience?
▶ How closely does the site's design mesh with the company's overall brand?

Once you evaluate your Top Five Sites, making note of what you like as well as what annoys you, check your site to see how it measures up. Which things are you doing right and which do you need to change or improve? By comparing your site with those sites you admire, you'll start to form a picture of where you want your site to go. Does one of your favorites have excellent articles, while your site is lacking in this area? Put that on the list. Do you frequently visit a site known for its great photography? Make yourself a note to improve the quality of images on your site.

In going through your Top Five Sites to determine what you like about them, you will form a great wish list for your site. As we work through the chapters to come, you'll be able to implement these wishes to make your site the best it can be.

# REAL LIFE >>
## *Bob's Favorite Sites (and Yours!)*

AT MY URGING, Bob visits the Top Ten Online Retailers list on GrokDotCom and says he will check back monthly to see who's moving up in the ranks (and what they're doing). The month that he checks, Office Depot is number one, and he notes the clear architecture and design that is prominent on that site. No wonder they have such a high conversion rate—they have some really compelling calls to action (like $20 off purchases of $75 or more, two free reams of paper when you buy toner, and free shipping). "Calls to action" are clever things on the site that get you motivated to act right now. Go to www.officedepot .com to observe their handiwork.

So how does the Top Five exercise apply to Bob? Well, as it turns out, Bob is a devoted indie music and film fan and he buys a lot of stuff on eBay. In fact, he visits the auction giant almost every day. In order to get ideas for his site, Bob takes a half hour or so to write down what he finds so appealing about the sites he uses every day.

Check out what Bob (and I) had to say about his Top Five Sites.

## The New York Times
*www.nytimes.com*

Good choice, Bob! The *New York Times* site is appealing because of its clean layout, constantly updated content, and consistently good writing. Also, it has a robust classified advertising section and great photography. Though it's a little heavy on the banner ads for my taste, Bob really likes the large amount of content offered by the *Times* online, so he marks it down as a plus.

What Bob likes most about this site is the clearly laid-out sections. He puts "Clear sections" on his list of things he wants to integrate into his site. Bob also notes that he would never find a typo on the *New York Times* site, so he makes a note to have his most grammar-obsessive friend go over his site.

## Harris Ranch
*www.harrisranchbeef.com*

Bob loves steak, and often places orders on the Harris Ranch site. What Bob likes the most about the site is the extremely clear access to customer service, both in email form and via an 800 number, right on the homepage. He notes that whenever he's used this information to contact the customer service department, he's always gotten either an immediate answer (on the phone) or an answer within forty-eight hours (by email). He notes that he's been less than diligent with his own customer service emails, though he is really good about answering and returning phone calls to the store.

Going forward, Bob will make his customer service information readily available on the website and will make more of an effort to build customer loyalty through good customer service, even if it means hiring a part-time employee to handle email inquiries and the mailing list. Great!

\* \* \*

## eBay
*www.ebay.com*

Bob collects vinyl records and other rock memorabilia, and so he visits eBay often to check for deals. EBay is mostly text, with virtually no design elements and only a few featured ads in the center. This site used to be much denser and more cluttered, but it has become more streamlined as the years have gone by, even as it has grown to feature millions of items. EBay is a great testament to the power of hierarchical organization.

Not only is Bob absolutely justified in his admiration of eBay (they have millions of users all over the world and continue to grow every year), but they might even be able to help him sell product and expand his business, as they now have many tools to help both small and large businesses of all types sell their products online. I recommend that he form an Amazing HomeMade Biscuits store on eBay to increase sales and drive traffic back to his site.

What Bob likes most about eBay is its great search functionality, and he wonders how to get a similar search on his site. Because I usually recommend against small businesses using up their budget to develop their own search tools, I suggest integrating one of Google's fine tools, but only after Bob puts some more content on the site.

Using what he likes about eBay as an example, Bob gets some inspiration for redesigning his own site. Next time, he decides, he's going to have a good search tool and cut down on the number of images. He also starts reading up on starting an eBay store to expand his site's reach.

## Zappos
*www.zappos.com*

Bob buys all of his shoes from Zappos. He likes them because their site is easy to navigate, they provide great customer service, and they have a lenient return policy. I have to agree; when you think about how hard it must be to sell shoes on the Internet (most people like to try on shoes, so automatically you're at a disadvantage), you'll understand why they have to be this good.

Incidentally, Zappos.com is so well-designed that it's easier to find shoes there than in an actual shoe store. Who would've thought?

What can Bob take from the example of Zappos.com? For one, he again notices that customer service is a very important part of helping this online business survive and thrive, so he puts a star next to "Improve customer service" on the to-do list for his site. Bob also remembers that the Zappos site offers a Free Shoe Giveaway and realizes that a giveaway campaign would be a great way to build a mailing list. He adds "Amazing HomeMade Biscuits Giveaway" to his list.

## Pandora
*www.pandora.com*

Bob plays cool music in his dog day care/store, and frequently finds out about new bands and songs by using Pandora, a personalized online radio service. He loves it because of its cool, simple design and the intuitiveness of its "Music Suggestion" interface, and because it's totally, completely focused on music (unlike Amazon or iTunes, where DVDs and electronic stuff distract him). He likes that every time he goes there, he learns something new.

Bob knows that when he goes to Pandora, he's just going to think about music and nothing else, and he finds this to be a welcome relief from the chaos of other websites. Going forward, Bob will take the example of Pandora and remove everything that's not dog-related from his site. Next time a friend asks him to put an advertisement for something other than dog-related stuff on the site, he'll say, "Sorry, no can do; I'm protecting my market niche and building my brand equity." Okay, maybe only Bob and I (and you!) will know what this means, but his site will be more successful because of it.

So what have you found on your Top Five Sites list that you'd like to integrate into your site? Do you admire great writing? Design? Customer service? Clean navigation? Note all your favorite things about your Top Five; anything you really respond to, you should definitely try to incorporate.

Each person's Top Five list will lead its owner to different conclusions.

Mine indicates that I value simplicity, clear design, and good writing; every site I work on reflects these preferences. Bob places a high value on good searchability, customer service, and site structure, so he'll be more likely to focus his attention on those elements when creating his site. When you make your Top Five list, try to identify which traits all of your choices have in common. These are the elements that are most important to you and the ones that will enable you to differentiate yourself on the web.

# 5 Find Your Stats

Routinely check your site's performance statistics to find
out how well it is attracting and engaging users.

**N**ow that you've studied some of the top-ranking websites in your
field and others, it's time to turn your attention to how your own
site is performing, so that you can set your goals for improvement. Being
able to quantify the effectiveness of your website is just as important as
being able to gauge its quality and user-friendliness. So now, let's turn
our attention to finding and evaluating your site's performance statistics
and to analyzing the traffic on your site. We'll look at several key pieces
of information that will tell you how people are finding and responding
to your site and what you can change to increase your site's traffic and
improve its performance.

First, let's look at your site's statistics, or "site stats," as they are more
commonly called. These figures tell you how many visitors your site gets
and the average length of time they spend on your site. Your web hosting
company keeps a record of this information, and it's usually free for the
asking as part of your hosting package.

In some cases, you might be able to pay a small fee for a more
advanced traffic analysis of your site. This information will tell you
where your users are coming from and where they're going in your
site. All of this data is really important to know when you're trying to

improve your website. If your web host offers more detailed stats, get them, even if you have to pay for them; it will be well worth it in the long run. Take some of the money you were going to use on marketing and spend it on a thorough site performance/traffic analysis instead (or first).

# Where to Check

There are several simple ways to find the statistics for your website. If you have a tech person or someone who works on your site for you, ask her or him for a printout of the site statistics for the last six months. This will give you some interesting trend data for the site and put you in control of the situation.

If you don't have a tech person or if you work on your website yourself, call your website hosting company to find out where they keep your site stats. Site stats are probably included with your website hosting package; they're usually built into your existing site and can be accessed with a simple URL, such as www.yoursite.com/stats. Try to get the most detailed version possible, even if you have to pay to upgrade your account. I recommend GoDaddy as a hosting company (www.godaddy .com). They are very responsive, professional, and inexpensive, and offer a multitude of services, including a great traffic measurement program called Traffic Facts.

Comprehensive site statistics are vital to measuring the effectiveness of your website. If you haven't been tracking this information, don't dismay. Just contact your web hosting company and find out how to access it, and then access and analyze these stats from this point forward. It will take at least one month to gather enough data to see how your site is performing, but it's better late than never, and once you do have this information, it will be very helpful to you.

Bookmark your site stats page for future access. You'll want to pay close attention to these statistics from now on; they're your record of who's doing what on your site. Check your stats at least once a week, if not daily. You want to know what's working, so you can do more of it.

## Google Analytics
*www.google.com/analytics*

Google is always in the process of developing great tools for web development, and Google Analytics is no exception. Google makes it easy to track everything from who's visiting your site to where they're coming from (and of course, how many of them are converting into customers). Google Analytics is free and easy to set up, and they have an in-depth tutorial to answer all your questions. If you're not using something to measure your traffic, this is a great place to start.

Here's how to get Google Analytics to start measuring your traffic right away:

1. Go to www.google.com/analytics, create an account, and register your site.
2. Copy the code that Google Analytics generates for you and save it to a Word document, which you can easily refer to in the future.
3. Paste this code into *every page* you want measured, to ensure the accuracy of your statistical readings. Site Meter (www.sitemeter.com) has very clear instructions for this based on what software you use to update your website. See the "Help" section for details.
4. Re-publish your site, or post the edited pages onto the server (however you get updates onto your site).
5. Log in to Google Analytics frequently to view your statistics. The more you track your stats, the more you'll learn about what works and what doesn't. And the more you know, the more power you have.

# What to Check

The following are a few important numbers you'll want to check at least weekly. Checking these statistics on a regular basis will give you valuable information, such as what pages are really popular, which ones people leave really quickly (indicating that you should beef up the content on that page), and where your traffic is coming from. Think of the statistics report as the thermometer for your site. The more you know, the more you can be proactive about refining the site so that it draws and retains more traffic.

If you've never heard some of these terms (like "unique visitors") before, don't be too concerned—you'll get the hang of the lingo once you find out where your stats actually live, or subscribe to a service that measures these things. If you find that your statistics do *not* include these measurements, I would be all means suggest adding (free) Google Analytics to your site, so you'll have the full scoop on your site traffic and visitors.

## Unique Visitors

This number is widely thought to be the only one that really matters, since hits can be affected by so many variables and the page views number is hard to decipher. "Uniques," as they're called, measure the number of individual users that came to your site during a certain time period (your traffic).

Simply put, the more uniques you have, the better. If the number seems low right now, don't worry. Once you begin to really improve your site's usability and do some simple marketing, this number will increase substantially.

## Average Visit Length

This tells you, on average, how long each person stays on your site. If your average visit length is less than five minutes, it usually means that people are not engaged with what they're seeing on your site and you need some new content. In order to achieve ten minutes or higher, you will need a full repertoire of interesting and pertinent content.

What's the point of getting people to spend more time on your site? The longer they stay, the more likely they are to buy something, click through to advertising or affiliate sites, and remember your brand. However, if people can see that all you want is to sell them something, they're not going to stay. The key is to engage them with good content that makes them feel like you're a trusted source of current, accurate information that's relevant to them. Visit length will give you an indication of how well your site's content engages your users. The more compelling your content is to your target audience, the more likely they are to regard you as an authority on your subject, take your suggestions seriously, buy your products, and return to your site to see what else you have to offer.

### Repeat Visitors

This stat is a record of how many of your users are coming back for a second (or third) time. This is a running figure that is calculated month by month and aggregated over the year. Increasing this number is key to building your business. Ideally, you want at least 30 percent of the total users on your site to be repeat visitors. I'll give you more strategies for encouraging people to return in later chapters, but for now let me emphasize this: If you give them a high-quality first experience, they will become repeat visitors. If this number is low, it most likely means that something about your site is making people not want to come back.

### Popular Pages Visited

Your site performance statistics should include a record of exactly how many times each page was visited. Your homepage should be listed as the first most popular, since most users will go to the homepage first to decide where else they want to go. If your homepage is not a frequently visited page, change the content to make it more engaging. If you see that thousands of people are visiting one of your sub-pages, consider replicating some of that content on your homepage. By visiting that page more than your homepage, users are telling you that your good content is buried. If you've got something that's working, don't hide it. Give users what they want up front!

### Referring URLs

This list will tell you which sites are linking to yours, which search engines have picked you up, and where you're located on the sites of your partners and affiliates. You can even click through on these URLs to see exactly where your link is placed and where all the traffic is coming from.

This information will come in handy in later chapters on promotion and marketing and search engine placement. For now, just make sure you can get this data easily and quickly.

## Google PageRank

Another good thing to know about your site is its Google PageRank (PR), if it's got one. You can tell this by downloading the Google Toolbar and looking at your site through it.

The Google Toolbar is also a cool little tool for measuring how successful your competitor's sites are, because PageRank applies to every site on the Internet. To do this, go to http://toolbar.google.com and click on "Download the Toolbar." The Google Toolbar will download itself right into your browser.

**What is PageRank, exactly?** This is one of those "less information is better" subjects. Here is the official definition, from Wikipedia (www.wikipedia.com):

> PageRank is a link analysis algorithm used by the Google Internet search engine that assigns a numerical weighting to each element of a hyperlinked set of documents, such as the World Wide Web, with the purpose of "measuring" its relative importance within the set.

**What?** Now, here's the extremely boiled-down version: When you look at your site through the Google Toolbar, it gives you a PageRank (PR) of X out of 10 (for example, 6/10). The higher the number, the more relevant your site. You'll also find this indicated, corresponding to the PageRank number, by a small green bar that looks a little like a gas tank, at the top of the Google Toolbar. Your site's Internet relevance corresponds to how "full" the green bar is, so look at it early and often. The Google Toolbar is the only place to measure your Google PageRank, so be sure to go over there and get it, just to increase your knowledge. This is supposed to measure where your site would appear on the results page if a user searched your business name or related terms.

**But how do you get a higher PageRank?** To get any PageRank with Google, your site needs to be listed with the Google search engine. (You'll learn how to list your site in Chapter 16.) This is not one of the paid Google AdWords campaigns that will be discussed in Chapter 17. What I'm talking about here is the actual Google directory, or the results that appear in the main area of Google when users type in search terms.

To increase your PageRank, your site has to be linked with other sites that have been picked up by Google and appear in their non-paid search listings. The higher your site's PageRank, the more often it will appear in Google's results, and the more often it appears in Google's results, the higher your site's PageRank will be. Talk about a classic catch-22!

**Confused?** For now, suffice it to say that this is a good way to measure how your site is doing in the wide world of the web right now, today. If your current PR is 0/10, don't stress about it. Once you've put some good content on your site and submitted your site to the search engines, your PR will start to rise, and your revenue along with it.

# REAL LIFE >>
## *Bob Checks His Site Stats*

BOB DIDN'T EVEN know he had site stats, so he was happy to call his hosting company and ask if they were keeping these for him. Bob uses a generic hosting service recommended to him by a former coworker, and they provide a pretty lackluster version of site statistics—just server requests and requests for pages. Since these stats only indicate overall hits and since one unique visitor could generate hundreds of hits, this doesn't really tell Bob much, except that people are somehow finding and going to his site and that his traffic has been about the same for the past six months.

According to the Google Toolbar, Bob's site has a PageRank of 2/10. This is pretty low, and probably means he's getting some traffic from the search engines when people type in "dog supplies" or any other of Bob's keywords. The ranking isn't bad, but the more he works on his site, the more traffic he's going to get, and the higher it's going to rank. Bob should be aiming for at least a 6/10 ranking, which he will be able to achieve within the year if he really works hard at improving and promoting the site and getting some relevant links back to it.

Just so you know, a hit is generated whenever a piece of content (images, files, or web pages) is downloaded to your computer. If the web page in question has many different images, pieces of technology, and other components, a single visit to that one page could be counted as several hits. What Bob needs to know is how many unique visitors he gets every month, where they come from, and how long they're staying. Knowing the number of hits to the site isn't going to tell him that.

About the only thing of interest in the general tracking is a "referring URL" report, which indicates to me that very few of Bob's users came to his site from another URL, leading me to conclude that the majority came directly to his site either by typing in his URL or, if they're a returning visitor, from a bookmark.

This means that many of his users probably learned of his site from a source other than a search engine or another website. Maybe they found out about the site after visiting his store, or through traditional (non-Internet) advertising or marketing, or by word of mouth. However they got there, it wasn't through an online source. That is not necessarily a bad thing, because clearly some of his marketing strategies are helping to get people to his site. But using search engines and links with other sites to increase his online exposure, in addition to his other marketing efforts, will increase the total volume of traffic to his site. The higher the number of visitors directed to his site from other URLs, the higher his site's search-engine rankings will be—and the higher his site's ranking, the more traffic will be directed to his site.

First and foremost, Bob needs more (and better quality) info about his visitors, so I suggest that he immediately switch over to Google Analytics, and then I walk him through opening an account and make sure he's put the measurement code in the right place on each of his pages. The first time he logs in, Bob is able to see how many unique visitors he's getting to his site, how long they're staying, and which URLs they're coming from. These statistics will allow Bob to see the results of his efforts and to track progress, which will motivate him to improve the site even more.

Now that you've got an idea of the traffic coming to your site (or a new way to measure it), you'll be able to watch, month by month, as the numbers grow. Looking at your site traffic and performance numbers on a regular basis is a great way not only to see the results of your efforts, but is also a way to keep yourself motivated to work on the site. Site stats are just another tool in your growing toolbox of web development that's going to make your site great. So make sure you know where to find this info again, and let's move on.

Next you'll learn how to gather and interpret your sales stats and customer feedback. All of this data forms the foundation upon which you'll redesign (or build) your website.

# 6 Gather Up Your Feedback and Do Some Tests

Knowing what your users think about and do with your site is just good business.

**Y**ou have a handle on how many people are finding your site (and how long they're staying there), so let's dig a little deeper and figure out how many of them are becoming your customers. For, as the saying goes, when you know better, you do better. That adage certainly applies to your site's conversion rate—the percentage of casual visitors that convert to paying customers—and to users' opinions of your site. The next step in your discovery process, beyond the site statistics even, is to gather and evaluate the sales data and as much customer feedback about your site as you can muster. This information will help you even more as you begin to construct your new site, as it will tell you what's working (and what's not) about your existing web presence. For instance, if you have a particular "call to action," like a two-for-one offer or a bestselling product call-out that's really prominent in the data, put that on the list of "things to keep." If you find you have a page that no one ever goes to or that people are complaining about, definitely put that on your list of things to leave behind.

So where to look for this golden information? Well, you can start by looking back at the history of sales on your site. Looking at your sales statistics (or sales stats) will give you a clear picture of what's selling and what's not, so you can further hone your ideas of what you customers really want and hopefully give them more.

# Homing In on Your Sales Stats

To borrow another adage: You can't know where you're going unless you know where you've been. Now is the time to gather up the current sales information for your site, so that you can get a clear picture of your baseline and set some goals for improvement. After all, you don't want to put in all this effort, only to be unable to tell if your numbers are going up.

You should collect and evaluate your sales data on a regular basis, at least monthly, if not weekly. You'll want to determine the following information.

## *Conversion Rate*

This is the percentage of your visitors who actually become customers. To find this number, divide the number of sales for a given period (day, week, month, quarter, or year) by the volume of traffic (number of unique visitors) for that same period. For example: If you average 100 sales per month and your site averages 5,000 uniques per month, your site's conversion rate is 2 percent ($5,000 \div 100 = .02$). This means you need 500 visitors to your site before you can expect to make one sale. If you've switched over to Google Analytics, they can also track your conversion rate for you.

There has been a great deal of debate over what constitutes an average conversion rate. I've seen everything from 1 percent to as high as 25 percent (with a lot of repeat visitors). According to a June 2008 survey conducted by Nielsen//NetRatings, the industry-wide average conversion rate for online retail sites is 3.9 percent. According to this survey, ProFlowers.com ranked number one, with a conversion rate of 28 percent. What should yours be? This is the one point on which virtually everyone agrees: The higher the conversion rate, the better.

It is important to note that increasing the traffic to your site alone is unlikely to increase your conversion rate. In fact, increasing your traffic without first improving the user experience on your site will probably cause your conversion rate to decrease, because an even higher volume of visitors will go to the site—only to turn around and leave without buying anything or using your site for its intended purpose, and with no plans to return. The best way to increase your conversion rate is to improve your site's usability and content before doing anything to drive more visitors to it. The longer users stay on your site and the more they use it, the more likely they are to convert to customers . . . and to become repeat customers.

## Pinpoint Your Bestselling Product

Obviously, you can tell this by the volume of the item sold on your website. Take note of where and how each top-selling item is positioned on your site, and then make it as easy as possible for all users to find and buy (or use) these items. If your best seller isn't already on your homepage, put it there.

Case in point: I once did some consulting on the website of a small computer hardware company that specialized in laptop computers. In their physical stores, laptops outsold all their other products combined; the word "laptops" was even in their company tagline. Although they had a strong brand off-line, their online presence was very generic, and amazingly, they did not have a single laptop on the homepage. The moral of the story: If you're known for something, don't make it hard for your users to find it. When you've got something customers obviously want from you (hence, it is your top sales item), put it on the homepage.

## Slow-Moving Items

If you offer a variety of products, you'll want to keep track of the sales volume of each item you carry. If one category of products or a specific item is more or less popular than the others, look at where and how it is presented on your website. If you have an item or a product line that is not selling well (or not at all), you might want to give it less prominent placement on your site and move better sellers to that space. Or you might want to rethink and change not only where but also *how* the product is presented on your site. Is it difficult to find? Is the navigational path from item to purchase clear and unobstructed? Does the product fit with your overall brand? Is the content, both the words and the image (if you have one), concerning this product compelling and appropriate for the target market? If there is no image, would including one help?

If you've done everything you can to properly position the item on your site and it still doesn't sell, it could be that the product is simply inappropriate for your target market. If that's the case, you can either have a fire sale to get rid of the inventory quickly or put it on eBay.

## Repeat Customers

Do you have an effective way of measuring return visitors to your site and their ordering habits? If you're using an online shopping cart/merchant account service (such as Yahoo! Business), they will definitely have these statistics for you. If your site doesn't take credit cards, just make identifying any matching names/orders part of your weekly sales data collection and evaluation, and create a database or Excel spreadsheet to keep track of this information.

Why is this important? Because repeat customers are your bread and butter, and they should be treated as such. Knowing and being responsive to your customers' wants, needs, likes, and dislikes will keep them coming back for more. Use every available strategy to increase your volume of repeat customers and every available means to appease them. There are many ways to reach out to your steady customers. For instance, would they like to be on a monthly subscription program for a specific product or product line? Would they like to hear about special offers or receive coupons? Do you have a physical mailing list of customers and prospects with whom you consistently communicate? If so, do you also have their email addresses? If not, we will start capturing those in Chapter 7.

If you have a content-only site or sell services or products that cannot be measured, these numbers obviously aren't as important to you. However, any time you notice one of your users coming back for more, so to speak, in the way of renewed subscriptions or even by way of repeated email comments or inquiries from the same person, make sure to put this person on a special preferred customer list. This person wants to buy what you are selling!

# Tuning In to User Feedback

It is a good idea to save and to periodically evaluate any and all emails pertaining to users' experiences with and opinions of your site. When people actually write to compliment you or to complain about something with your site, take that opportunity to make them your customers. Think of it this way: They cared enough about you to find your contact information and to use it. They clearly want to do business with you; give them every reason to do just that—even if it means making your site better in order to win (or win back) their confidence. No matter what they say—even if it is something as crass as "Your site totally sucks!"—your response should be positive, something like "Thank you for your email. We continually strive to make our site better. Can you tell us what you don't like about it?" Maybe one person's pet peeve is broken links, and that person has found three on your site. Maybe another person is offended because you don't have enough men on your site, or minorities, or dogs, or cats, or whatever. Try to find a kernel of good information in every negative comment, and you'll consistently improve your site.

Customers that love your site and use it often might take issue with changes you make—whether to the site's design, features, or product offerings. More rarely, other users will take it upon themselves to offer positive feedback, in which case you should always personally thank them for their interest . . . and then ask them to tell you, specifically, what they like best about your site. While you're at it, you might also ask them what they think could be improved.

Don't get me wrong: I am not suggesting that you engage in lengthy debates with complete strangers about the choices you've made on your website. However, if you can find out what the user's specific beef or preference is, you at least have a meaningful piece of information that you can use to assess the situation. What you choose to do (or not to do) with this information is always up to you. Design decisions, word selections, and choices about the thrust of your overall message are yours alone to make.

Though it can sometimes be difficult to hold your tongue and not to send a fervently defensive email in reply to a highly critical one, it is unwise to wage an electronic war of words over someone's opinion of your website. It is, after all, just one person's opinion. Whenever you put something on the Internet, where potentially millions of people can poke around (and poke holes through) it, you are bound to get at least a few unsolicited digs about your work. Take these comments for what they are—merely opinions—and don't overreact to negative feedback; doing so will only come back to haunt you.

On the other hand, feedback from your paying customers, qualified potential customers, and people who actively use your website is invaluable. Read their emails and posts (if your site features a bulletin board, blog, or similar feature), and then take their feedback into consideration when evaluating your website and making any changes to it.

## What You Know Can Help You

Studies show that as few as 4 percent of dissatisfied customers complain to the company with which they are unhappy. In the very best of circumstances, a mere 30 percent voice their complaints to a company. That means that 70 to 96 percent of unhappy campers never say a peep—to you, anyway. But they will tell seven to ten other people about their displeasure with your company.

With online businesses, it can be even worse. Numerous studies have shown that excellent service is the most important factor in online customer satisfaction. When online customers are ticked off about your site, not only will they tell the seven to ten people they regularly come into contact with, they might broadcast it to the world by posting it on their blog or any of the myriad online complaint sites out there. Plus, because of the immediate nature of the Internet, online customers tend to expect a faster response to their complaints.

Another startling reality is that more than two-thirds (63 percent) of dissatisfied customers never come back. That's a big chunk of lost business, when you consider that for most businesses, an average of 65 percent of their income comes from repeat business. At a time when brand loyalty is crucial to the success of any business, customer service can make, or break, an online enterprise.

As scary as all this might seem, customer complaints are actually a good thing. After all, you can't fix something if you don't know it's broken. If your site gets a decent amount of traffic and there's something amiss—a weird piece of technology that's not working, a broken link, an egregiously misspelled word—it's really only a matter of time before you get an email or two about it, if you haven't already. In that case, look at a user complaint as an opportunity to improve your site.

Also keep in mind that the majority of your users are probably satisfied with the site as it is and that no one expects absolute perfection. There is only so much you can do to prevent and resolve problems. Inevitably, something is going to slip through the cracks, and when it does, you'll deal with it. Just do what you can to avoid errors and to resolve them when you become aware of them.

Responding quickly, directly, and fully to user complaints will improve customer satisfaction. Sometimes it can even bring back a disgruntled customer. And it definitely will boost your sales.

## The Power of Proactivity

Don't get caught up in the mistaken notion that no news is good news. Just because you've received few or no complaints about your site doesn't mean all is well or even mostly well. Remember, the majority of dissatisfied customers never speak out—to you, anyway. Don't wait for bad news to make its way to your email inbox; instead, ask for it and be prepared to deal with it. The most successful online businesses are those that are proactive in providing easy-to-find and easy-to-use mechanisms on their websites that enable users to resolve potential glitches before they become annoying problems.

The following are a few of the most effective customer relations management tools you can build into your website:

**FAQs.** One way to nip user hassles in the bud up-front is to include a "Frequently Asked Questions" (FAQ) page on your site. This is a list of questions and answers about the nuts and bolts of how to use your site, place an order, determine the status of an order, return a purchase, report a broken link or technical problem, comment on the content, get one-on-one customer service, and the like.

If you decide to use an "FAQ" section, be sure to put it in a prominent place and to clearly and simply state your questions and answers.

**Direct Customer Service Links.** Studies show that people want to deal directly with people, especially when they have a question, concern, or problem. Studies also show that the faster your resolve a problem, the more likely you are to convert and keep that customer. So it is wise to include a customer service link on your site—and in a prominent position that customers can easily spot and then simply click on to "talk" with someone who can resolve their problem. I suggest setting up at least one unique email address or a fill-in-the-blank form for communicating customer service issues and sending them directly and immediately to someone (perhaps you) who can and will address the issue in a timely manner.

# Go Forth and Gather Your Users!

If you haven't already done this, there's no time like the present to gather up all of your customers' email addresses into your official mailing list. This includes everyone who's ever bought anything from you, asked for more information, or contacted you through your site in any way. If you're using a merchant account/shopping cart service, they should have all of the contacts saved; it's just up to you to get them. You can use an Excel spreadsheet or your Microsoft Outlook until your list gets too large, and then you'll need to switch to some easy-to-use contact management software. You might want to start with PHP List (www.phplist.com), which is free and easy to use. If you find that you need something with more features, some examples include Constant Contact (www.constantcontact.com), iContact (www.icontact.com), and GetResponse (www.getresponse.com). Each of these offers free trials and can help you gather up all your contacts in one place and keep in touch with your users. It's important!

## *Now Contact Them!*

Once you have your mailing list, send your contacts a short survey to see what they think of your site. Later, you'll use the list to announce your relaunch, to market products, and to keep in touch with your user base, but for now, let's find out what they like and don't like. Keep it short, simple, and professional, and survey sparingly; don't pester your users with repeated surveys. Ask for specific information about what might increase the users' satisfaction with and use of your site.

To thank them for providing you with this valuable information, you can offer some kind of giveaway or sweepstakes to everyone who submits a completed survey. Providing an incentive will usually boost the survey response rate.

Here is a sample survey:

To: My mailing list
From: me@me.com
Subject: We want to make your experience better!

Dear User Name,

We are in the process of redesigning our website to make the experience better for you, our loyal customer. Please take a minute to answer the following few questions:

1. Does anything on our site bother you? If so, please tell us what.
2. Has anything on our site not worked properly for you? If so, please tell us what.
3. Is there anything you'd like us to change? If so, please tell us what.
4. Would you like to receive our monthly newsletter?

Thank you for your participation in this survey. We value your feedback.

Sincerely,
My signature

\* \* \*

## *How User Feedback Shaped a Website*

I've been working on the site DiscoverNursing.com since 2001. Since I'm not a nurse, I obviously couldn't know all of the different specialties, organizations, and subjects that would be of interest to those in the nursing world. The very first version of the site (shown below) was structured around a simple why/how architecture, with all the major content grouped within these two buckets.

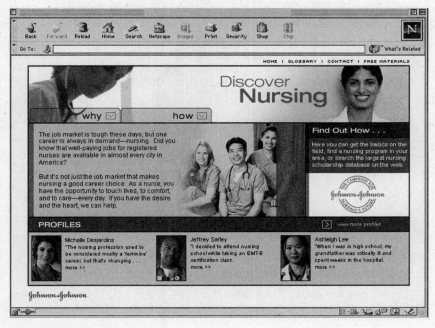

By Johnson & Johnson Services, Inc.

As the site grew and received feedback from nurses and nursing organizations, it was redesigned to accommodate the increased content. The "Contact," "Free Materials," and "Glossary" links are connected to the most popular sections of the site; these links stayed even when the site was redesigned.

During the site's first year, we received a lot of emails (about five hundred per month) about the site—questions, negative and positive feedback, and a wealth of suggestions for new content. For instance, people loved that we were promoting the nursing profession in general, but nurses pointed out that the original site didn't have a separate section for specialties such as oncology or pediatric nursing. The nursing community let us know that we should provide in-depth information on each subspecialty, as well as gave us hundreds of real-life profiles which we also incorporated.

By Johnson & Johnson Services, Inc.

As you can see above, in addition to the "Why" and "How" sections, we now have two whole new kinds of sections, "Who" and "What." The site also features more than one hundred sub-pages of nursing specialties, ranging from "Schools with No Waiting List" to "How to Become a Nurse Advocate." In the years the site has been up, it's gone from being a simple website supporting a national campaign to promote the nursing profession and address the nursing shortage in the United States to being the number one source for nursing information on the Internet (according to Google). This is a testament to the power of good content.

There is no better time than now, when you are preparing to design or redesign your website, to start collecting and analyzing all the information you can about how people find, view, and use your site. Gather up whatever user statistics you can find and all the customer feedback you've received about your site so far, and look for common themes. If you spot a recurring problem and it's easy to fix right then, fix it while the fixing's good. If people are repeatedly asking for the same thing, consider adding it during your site redesign. If you are receiving multiple compliments about certain features or notice heavy activity on certain pages, make sure to retain and, if possible, to enhance these strengths during the redesign.

# Conduct Focus Groups

Another great way to gather really specific information about what's working (and what's not) on your website is by conducting a focus group or two on your current site. Website focus groups are similar to and serve the same purpose as focus groups routinely conducted by advertising agencies and marketing experts: A bunch of people who are typical of the customers you're trying to reach are gathered together and asked to give their candid and personal impressions about a specific product. For larger companies, website focus groups are usually run by the in-house marketing and/or design departments or by a third-party testing organization or marketing consultant (again, for objectivity). Focus groups (and the firms that run them) can be costly, though (complete testing can easily run into the thousands), and I'm assuming you're going to want to spend any and all of your website budget on actually building a site and getting people to see it. So with that in mind, I'm here to tell you that many website owners do their own focus groups, and you can too.

## How to Do Your Own Focus Group

Just follow these few simple steps:

1. Invite five to ten of your most objective and candid friends and/or colleagues to a focus group meeting, specifying the date, time, place, and purpose.
2. Prepare a series of questions prior to the day of the focus group. (See the list of sample questions on page 74.)

3. Designate someone other than yourself as the group leader and provide him or her with clear instructions on how to conduct the focus group.

4. Set up the space with enough chairs and with whatever equipment and supplies might be needed, for example a video camera, paper and pens, bottles of water, and so forth. Make sure there's a computer in the room (or bring your own), with an Internet connection that works.

5. Once everyone is settled, have the leader bring up your website on the computer and then ask each of the questions you've prepared, one by one. The leader should encourage each participant to express his or her opinions and allow time for discussion among members of the group.

6. Record the results, either on video or audio or by taking written notes. It is best to have someone else record the session. If you do videotape, make sure to have participants fill out a release form (available on www.usability.gov). If you record the session yourself, do so discreetly and from the back of the room, and do not interact with the group. Even if you're just observing the session, stay out of the way (out of the room, if you can) and do not interact. After all, you want the group's objective opinions—the way they would respond to your site in their own environments and without anyone looking over their shoulders—which you're not likely to get when you participate or when your presence is dominant.

7. Take a walk. People can be harsh, even people you know. Before you try to figure out the meaning of what the focus group has said, take a walk to get some perspective. You've probably just heard more comments about your site all at once than in its whole history, and it's going to take some time to digest.

8. Review the results. Later, when your head is clear, review the tape and/or the notes from the focus group for the valuable insights, impressions, and comments provided by the group. While this might be painful, it will certainly be informative and give you a clear idea of the areas of your site that need work. Did members of the group react negatively to the design or the content? Did

they think the site was for something other than its intended purpose? Did they "get" it? If any of these issues came up, be sure to either address them in your site right away or add them to your list of things to change if you're currently in the beginning or middle of a redesign.

If you don't have enough friends and colleagues willing to participate in your focus group, or if you don't trust their opinions, or if they are totally outside your market demographics, put an ad on Craigslist or in your local newspaper for focus group participants. If your site is targeted toward young people, you might want to advertise at a local community college or university. For example, if I were conducting a focus group for a new website that sold baby products online, here's an example of an ad I might place:

### Focus Group Participants Needed

I am conducting a focus group for a new website. Participants should be between the ages of 30 and 40, have young children, and not work at an Internet design or development company. Pay is $50 for two hours. Email for more information: me@me.com.

Why, you might be wondering, is it important that focus group participants not work at an Internet design or development company? In my experience, I have found that people who make websites for a living have trouble being objective. Once you've created umpteen sites, you tend to focus too much on the nitty-gritty issues of programming, design, usability, and so on, and not enough on the overall impressions of the site. It is more beneficial to assemble a focus group of people who fit the demographic profile of your users (which Chapter 2 helped you define).

And, why pay them $50 for two hours? you might ask. Perhaps this seems like a lot, when all they're doing is telling you what's wrong with your website. Well, yes—you probably aren't going to enjoy hearing all they're thinking, but the $50 at least guarantees that you'll get some well-educated, intelligent people who might consider a paid focus group worth their time and who are really representative of your target demographic. You need to at least make it worth their while if you're going to ask them to give you their undivided attention and honest opinions for two hours. Don't skimp on the focus group. Then again, don't overpay them, either—you don't want them to like you too much.

Comb through the resumes you receive, make a list of your likely candidates, and then give them a call or an email to scope them out. You're looking for high-quality people who can articulate their opinions (and not just people looking to make fifty bucks), because the opinions you get at this stage of the game could save you hundreds (perhaps thousands) of dollars in the long run. These are the insights you're going to use to create a website that is truly indicative of your brand and business.

When you ask people to give their honest opinions of your site and then get out of their way so they feel free to actually voice them, you might be surprised at what they say—and at how useful their input is. If you watch a focus group from the other side of a one-way window, as some site owners do, you might find yourself cringing every time someone says they don't "get" what you think is a perfectly clear image, they just don't like a headline you wrote, or they can't find anything even though you think it's laid out perfectly clearly. But listen anyway—and see what you can learn.

## What to Ask Your Focus Group

Typical focus group questions include:

▶ Do you get the point of this website?
▶ What is the main product or service that this company sells? What else do they provide? Can you tell just by looking at the site?
▶ What feelings do you associate with this company, based on the website?
▶ Where would you go on this site if you needed to contact customer service?
▶ Do you think the sections are clearly laid out? Would you have an idea of what content you might find under each heading, without clicking?

▶ Do you think the website maintains the look and feel of the company's off-line advertising and marketing collateral?

▶ Would you have faith in this company based on your overall impression of this website?

▶ Do you see anything on this site that seems outdated, makes the site look cheap or amateurish, or just looks wrong?

## Conduct Usability Testing

Like focus group testing, usability testing also involves getting a group of people in a room and getting them to comment on your site, with the purpose of figuring out what's working and what isn't. The difference is that with usability testing, the people are given tasks to perform on your site, which they do while you (or a test leader) watch them and make notes. Usability testing can provide some of the most informative (if sometimes excruciating) information about the user-friendliness of your site, because it gives you a front-row seat as you watch people fumble, bumble, and navigate around it. For the record, formal usability testing is usually done by a professional firm; if you're interested and have the budget for this, I recommend checking out the website of the Nielsen Norman Group (www.useit.com). If you're just interested in a more informal picture of how your site is working, you can conduct the low-budget version of this yourself.

For usability testing, you'll need three or four participants. Why are there fewer people in usability testing than in a focus group? Unlike focus groups, usability testing is not a group exercise. Each person must perform the tasks individually, with no help from you or interaction with one another, while you (or a test administrator) observe and take notes (or videotape). For this reason, usability testing conducted by only one person happens over the course of a whole day, with approximately two hours allocated for each participant. If you have too many participants, you'll end up with more information than you can practically use, and the testing process will take far too long. So get out your video camera, stick to watching three to four people actually complete tasks on your site, and you'll get a wealth of information you can use to further refine it.

## How to Conduct a Usability Test

Here are some general instructions for running some simple usability testing of your website yourself, on a low budget. For more extensive information, visit www.usability.gov/refine/learnusa.html.

1. Invite three or four trusted friends/colleagues to be your usability testers or run an ad for testers on Craigslist or in your local paper.

2. Create an instruction script that indicates how the test will be run, informs participants that they will be videotaped, and so forth. Again, make sure to have participants fill out a release form (available on www.usability.gov).

3. Create a list of tasks to be tested, based on what you want to know about your site. For usability testing, make sure to design tasks that involve interaction with your site, such as "Find a product, and complete an order using the shopping cart" and "Find the Contact Us section, and send an email about the site" and "Find X product on the site."

4. Create a follow-up questionnaire, so that you can collect impressions, comments, and suggestions from each participant. Testers usually have opinions and like the opportunity to comment after the test. Make the questionnaire specific to the things you want to know about the site. You can even use the list of questions in the "What to Ask Your Focus Group" section, above, to get you started (or just use the whole list).

5. Make all other necessary preparations, such as setting up the computer and the video camera, printing out release forms, and so on.

6. Instruct the testers to perform each task, one by one. Make sure you use the same script for each person, so the tests are identical; that way, you'll get the most useful information for purposes of comparison. Encourage subjects to tell you what they're thinking. You're looking for phrases such as "I don't understand what to do next," or "I don't know what this button does," or "Product X isn't where I thought it would be."

Testers can say things like this out loud (which will be captured on your videotape of the session), or you might just watch them try to complete a task and document how they did it. This is an action-oriented test; you want to see real people interacting with your live website, so you'll have an idea of what's happening when people are alone at home or at work or in whatever environment in which they would normally use a computer to access your site.

7. Observe quietly as each tester performs each function. Resist the urge to coach. You are not going to be there when people are using the site on their own in real life, so don't give the testers the answers to the questions, no matter how much it hurts you to watch them. Be kind and patient. Even though the site might be your baby and you've spent the last year writing every word yourself, be open-minded and watch without comment. Remember, you are trying to get a bird's-eye view of what people will be doing on your site. During the testing process, users should be discouraged from asking questions. In fact, it's better if they pretend you're not there at all. After each test, give users the questionnaire so that they can give you their overall impressions.

# REAL LIFE >>
## *Bob Gets the Scoop*

BOB'S CLIENT LIST has been steadily building for the past couple of years. He's got a good mailing list of people that visit his physical locations, and he sometimes does mailings to the list to announce sales, give out coupons, or send a newsletter. Bob's site, however, has been up for about a year, and it's just not taking off the way Bob would like. The conversion rate for visitors who become customers is about 2 percent, which is below the industry average, and Bob knows if the site worked better, more of his regular customers would order products online and refer their friends.

Bob's email address is on the site (in the "Contact Us" section), and one question he gets all the time is "Where can I find those biscuits?" To me, this indicates that Bob should move the biscuits to where they can easily be located, both now and for his future site.

Bob admits that he's never really done any testing of his site, short of clicking around himself to see if the links work. All he's really got is the informal survey he did of his friends (who agreed that they didn't really "get" the site and found it kind of messy-looking). I suggest doing one focus group, just so Bob can get a feel for users' impressions of the site.

Bob agrees, and places an ad and gets four smart, dog-loving people who match his target audience. One Saturday afternoon, his volunteer testers run his site through a series of tasks and tell him what they think. Because we don't have a huge budget, I videotape the users one at a time as they follow the same set of instructions.

When all is said and done, Bob takes what he's learned from the group testing experience, combines this with the statistical information and sales data we've collected before, reviews his original goals for his new site (to build sales and community as well as create a site that better reflects his in-store brand), and prepares for the redesign. First, though, we're going to get in there and fix some of the big errors on his existing site, so that he can at least get it working better and feel better about having it out there while we're working on the new stuff. Every little bit helps!

# 7 | Triage

Use this emergency triage for diagnosing and treating your website's most obvious afflictions . . . right now.

Once you've got the scoop on how your site is doing, I'm sure you'll be dying to apply some of your newfound knowledge to your own site. Let's jump-start your website makeover by putting it through a diagnostic triage and checking it for some of the most common usability problems on the World Wide Web today. Since people tend to just avoid sites that don't work for them without so much as a single word to the site's owner, you might not even know that these website boo-boos are annoying your users . . . and hurting your business. But if your site suffers from any of these ailments, it is probably the reason why users aren't spending more time there and actually using it. Correct just a few of these problems and you will drastically improve your site's user experience rating. Your customers will thank you. Your business will thank you. I will thank you.

In addition to (or instead of) the problems mentioned in this chapter, you could go to your focus group/usability testing results and your user feedback, and fix the cosmetic problems that people mentioned the most, like broken links or typos. If, like Bob's website, your site suffers from one or more of these problems, don't get worried or overwhelmed. Really, you could leave everything the way it is now and still be fine, since we're heading into the "Design and Development" section next, where everything is spelled out step by step. So just look over the list for now, but even if your site has every problem mentioned, it's still going to be okay. You've done so much good work already, and you're well on your way to complete website domination. Of course, if I can get you to pull some typos or broken links off of your site, too, that would be just great.

# Biggest Website Offenders

So here's a list of the biggest website offenders, which a few of my favorite web development professionals and I have collected. Some are controversial, some are funny, and some are downright horrible. Luckily, some of them are really easy to fix (like removing broken links or things that download right from the homepage), and will be a great first step in improving your usability.

### Free and Obscure URLs

At this point in the history of the Internet, registering your site is easy enough and cheap enough that you should *never* run your business on a free internet service provider (ISP) or submit a site built on a free ISP (like the free sites offered by Tripod or Angelfire, both Lycos companies, or by GeoCities) to the search engines. Pay the extra fee for a "dedicated" URL and hosting service from the beginning—you will not be sorry! Here's why: No matter how great a site might be, if it's got a long URL with four slashes in it, no one is going there. They're certainly not going to type in a gigantic URL, and even if your site does somehow manage to show up in a search engine's results, the users' opinions of your site (and your business) will go down the second they see it's got a "free" URL. They are less likely to click on, much less do business with, a freebie (read, amateur) URL than a unique (read, professional) URL that the site owner paid for. Why would a user take your online business seriously and actually buy something from your site if you can't invest the $50 to get your own URL and web-hosting package? Do yourself a big favor and get a respectable web address. If you don't know how to do this, follow these simple steps at an all-in-one place like GoDaddy.com, which can offer you the URL, hosting, and even the design for one low price. Depending on the size and scope of your site, you should be able to move it from a free URL to a dedicated URL (such as www.mysite.com) fairly quickly, and you will start to see results right away. Here's how:

1. Choose a good name for your website. Each web address consists of the same prefix (http://www.), followed by a unique domain name that you create, and then your choice of a variety of suffixes, such as ".com," ".net," ".org," and the like. (See #3, below, for more information on suffixes.) Since there's a good chance that another site may have already reserved your first choice, it's a good idea to choose several different domain names for your web address. So take a few minutes to jot down several possibilities on a piece of paper. Your domain name should be as short and simple as possible. It should also be easy to remember and relate to your business in a way that users will recognize. Don't use a hyphen (-) or underline (_); these create a much higher margin of error when the user tries to type in your address. You want to make it as easy as possible for people to find you.

2. Go to a name-registration service, like GoDaddy (www.godaddy .com) or Register.com (www.register.com).

3. Type in the web address you want (www.mywebsite.com, for example). Remember, you will have the option of reserving your domain name under any one of several suffixes (.com, .net, .org, and so on). For most businesses, your first choice should be .com, which designates a commercial site; the next best choice would be .net. If the site is for a nonprofit organization, .org would be the ideal suffix; for an educational institution's site, it would be .edu. Alternate suffixes such as .biz and .tv and country codes (.us and .ca) are slowly catching on, but aren't quite memorable enough yet to build your whole business around. Getting one of these suffixes now, when they are not widely recognized and used, increases the likelihood that someone might remember the name of your URL but forget the suffix. For instance, let's

say your new URL is www.ilovecats.tv. The "I love cats" part is catchy and memorable, but most users will automatically type in www.ilovecats.com, because they're accustomed to URLs that end with .com. They might not even be aware there is a .tv suffix. If there is another site out there with the URL www.ilovecats .com, you will have inadvertently driven more traffic to your competition. Choosing an equally memorable and catchy name but with a .com suffix would be more beneficial to you.

4. The registration site will instantly tell you whether the web address (URL) you typed in is available. If your first choice has already been reserved by another site, keep typing in the names you came up with earlier until you get one that is available and you can live with.

5. Follow the registration site's online instructions for setting up an account to host your site on their server. Make sure to have your payment information (usually, a credit or debit card) ready to enter; you usually need to pay at least the first month of hosting in advance and then commit to monthly payments thereafter.

6. Take the content from your free site and make new pages. If you used a program like Dreamweaver or HomeSite to build the originals, copies of all the pages should work just fine. If not, use a simple program (like GoDaddy's "Website Tonight," www .godaddy.com) or the excellent "Homestead" product offered by Intuit (www.homestead.com). At this point you're not so much redesigning as just moving stuff from one place to another. Just doing this one thing will increase traffic to your site and give you an air of legitimacy.

## Things That Download Right from the Homepage

If you have a link on your homepage that launches a PDF (or other download) with no warning, please take it off. "Instant download" links make users think they did something wrong and now have a computer virus, and this will make them leave your site and never come back. If you're going to have them download something, put it on its own page, and make sure there are clear instructions for (a) how to download the actual file, and (b) where to get any software or additional technology they might need, such as Adobe Acrobat Reader, QuickTime, or Windows Media Player.

Under this heading I am also going to include the incredibly annoying "Contact Us" button that pops up a "mail to" or blank email form instead of a separate page. The "mail to" seems easy to use but is actually forcing your user's computer to open her or his email program to send you an email. But . . . what if the user is on someone else's computer? What if she or he doesn't want to open the email program right then? What if forcing the email program to open crashes the computer, and the user blames you? I think you can see where I'm going with this. What you want is a simple, easy-to-understand "Contact Us" page, either with an email address or a fill-in information form, and perhaps also a telephone number and street address. Any of these is going to get you much more feedback than the dreaded "mail to."

## Too Much Information on the Homepage

Also known among professional web developers as the "burden of too much choice," a bloated homepage means that the users are absolutely slammed with information when they first get to your site. If you make users choose between too many things right at the beginning, they often choose to leave. Just as you don't get a second chance to make a first impression in real life, you don't get a second chance to wow users with your website. Putting everything you have on your homepage is the equivalent of telling your blind date your entire life story, complete with all the intimate details of your previous romances and your deepest desires, the very first time you meet. Just as on an overloaded blind date, your users won't be able to get away from your site fast enough—and they aren't likely to come back for a second round of too much, too soon.

If your homepage extends significantly below the fold (beyond the first screen), it's got too much content and is probably overwhelming your users. Having to scroll excessively on a homepage to view all the content usually makes a website appear cluttered and disorganized. Users, especially first-time visitors to a site, tend to have a very low threshold for scrolling on homepages. So unless you're an established site where users expect tons of content on the homepage, like the *New York Times* or Salon.com, it is best to limit your homepage content to one screen in which you succinctly specify what your site offers and how users can access it, and then make it easy for users to dig deeper into your site from there. Williams-Sonoma does an excellent job of displaying 90 percent of their homepage content on a single screen (www.williams-sonoma.com). Having a clean, attractive, easy-to-use, and sharply focused homepage is one of the easiest ways to increase sales. Your first goal should be to clean up your homepage, removing everything that does not present your brand and guide users to do what you want them to do on your site. Make sure most (if not all) of your homepage content appears above the fold (on the first screen). For more on what to put on your homepage, see Chapter 13. For now, making a serious effort to de-bulk your homepage will pay off in the form of a higher conversion rate (first-time visitor to paying customer).

If the content you've removed from the homepage doesn't seem to fit anywhere else on your site, don't panic. We'll get to the nitty-gritty of website architecture in Chapter 8.

## Frames

This web-development holdover from the late nineties didn't work well then (which is why web developers stopped using and recommending it), and it is totally passé now. Yet, some people continue to use it. When you build a website in frames, the entire site is under one URL (frame), and every sub-page exists beneath it, so the URL never changes as you navigate through the site. One of the biggest problems with frames is that search engines cannot see these sub-pages or any of the content on them. If the search engine can't see your words, it's not going to find and list your website when people are searching for those words on the Internet. Worse, if your site is in a frame set, you won't be able to get accurate site statistics—meaning you'll have no idea who's coming to your site, how long they're staying, or whether any of your revamping efforts are working.

One other thing: Frames are a major user-experience faux pas. Having many sections under one address makes users feel lost, because as they move from page to page, they have no way of knowing where they are within the site. You never want to confuse and distract users by making them wonder, "What's happening? . . . I thought clicking on that button would take me to this page, but now I don't even know where I am. . . . Why didn't it work? . . . Is the page still under construction? . . . Is the site broken? . . ." If you take nothing else away from this book, take this: Once you lose the user, you'll have a hard time getting him back.

The solution for this frames problem is simple: Give each page of content its own URL. In a frames site, every page has the same URL—for example, www.mysite.com. In a non-frames site, each page has a unique URL, such as www.mysite.com/products.html, www.mysite.com/about .html, and so on. This might require creating a bunch of new pages in Dreamweaver or a similar program, but you should be able to copy and paste the content. Separate pages will allow your site to rank in the search engines, make it much easier for the user to navigate, and give you a clearer picture of what's working on your site. Unless and until you free the site from frames, you're never going to know what's working, who's coming, and what they're doing. Don't make *any* other changes if your site is still in frames. Focus all your energy on fixing this one problem, and you'll see a huge difference, both in usability and user satisfaction.

## No Way to Sign Up/Subscribe

In marketing circles, they say that a new customer has to be exposed to your product eight to ten times before he or she "converts" or becomes a new customer. Since you have about ten seconds to make your first impression when someone visits your site for the first time, it's going to be very difficult to achieve that number in just one visit.

The solution for this is just to put an opt-in box on your site that will allow people to join your mailing list, so you can send them updates or newsletters, new offers, or new articles you've written. Building your mailing list is easy and free, and so there's no reason for you not to be doing it. There are several free sites that will help you do this, including FeedBurner (www.feedburner.com) and PHP List (www.phplist .com), which work well for people with blogs or who make frequent updates to their sites. If you need more services and have a budget, try email-marketing "autoresponder" sites like Constant Contact (www .constantcontact.com) or GetResponse (www.getresponse.com), which will help you not only with capturing the email addresses, but marketing to your list once it's built up. The latter two services are free to use for capture, but once you start doing the actual marketing, they will charge you, either a small monthly fee or a fee per email "broadcast" (which is when you send email to everyone on your list). You will need to decide which service is right for you based on your needs, and a quick review of what these services have to offer can help you do that. I've also included a reference guide to these services in Chapter 18.

Each of these services offers a free trial, so I would recommend implementing some sort of email capture on your site right away. Think of it this way: If they like your site enough to sign up, it might only take a few emails from you until they end up becoming your regular customers. If you don't give them a way to do that, you are losing future sales. So get the email sign-up box. It's important!

As a word of caution: Because of new anti-spam and privacy laws, it is advisable to use an autoresponder service that allows people to "opt in" to your list and "opt out" anytime they want. This makes subscribing and unsubscribing easy for users—and easier on you. A service like this saves you from having to maintain an Excel spreadsheet of people's email addresses and having to manually remove people from the list individually. These email management services are cheap enough and easy enough that you should get one and use it for your website right away.

## Off-Strategy Content

Off-strategy content includes advertisements, articles, images, or anything else that doesn't cater to your target audience (now that you've defined who they are and what they want). If you have ads that are stealing attention from what you want your ideal user to do, remove them. If you have a fancy Flash intro on a site that's otherwise low-tech and targets middle-aged people, now's the time to get rid of it. We'll talk more (much more) about what to put on the site and where to put it, but for now (with your target audience in mind), just take a look at your site to see that it doesn't have anything that totally doesn't match.

Under this heading I am also going to include "music that plays on your site and can't be turned off," because I consider this to be off-strategy for all target audiences. No one, not even a kid who loves video games, wants to be forced to listen to your website's theme song over and over again while trying to find her or his way around your site. Many experts say that music on websites is slowly dying out anyway, but if you insist on having it (and, don't get me wrong— sometimes it actually does work), make sure there is a clear "Turn Off Music" button or link that appears on every page. For a good example of this, I would suggest visiting the official website of Tom Cruise (www.tomcruise.com), which makes good use both of music and of the turn-off-music function.

## Stuff That Doesn't Work

This is another big one, and makes a huge difference if you keep an eye out. I can't tell you how many companies I've consulted for that have more than one broken link, right on their homepage, that they don't know about but that has been annoying users (and making them look bad) for who knows how long. If nothing else, go to your site once a month and click everything that's clickable, make sure everything loads, and just eyeball it to see that everything is working the way it should. Maybe something broke and you don't know it. Maybe someone you're linking to went out of business. Maybe one of the images on your homepage mysteriously disappeared. Maybe . . . well, you get the point. Broken links are a sign of site neglect, and you want your customers to be totally confident that you're working hard for them. Working hard on your site is a good way to indicate this.

It is a great idea to run your site through one of these broken link checking programs periodically (at least every quarter), just to make sure you're not leading people into broken link land. Think of it as a multivitamin for your website. The free "broken link check" offered by either of these programs is fine: www.dead-links.com and http://validator.w3.org/checklink.

## *Web Counter*

With the site statistics programs now available, it is no longer necessary (and not always wise) to include a hits or visitors counting feature on your website. Statistics programs can provide great insight into how many people are visiting your site and how long they're staying, but this is information *you* need to know, not necessarily information you want to broadcast to the whole world. These statistics are measured on the back end of your site, and putting a counter on the part that people can see (the front end) just makes you look like you don't know what you're doing.

Worse, if you have a small volume of traffic at this point, a visible hit counter just shows your competition that they're doing better than you.

You'll find more information on site statistics programs in Chapter 5. There are much better programs than the hit counter, some of them free. For now, just lose the visible hit counter. It's bringing you down.

## *Too Much Design*

In designing your site, have you focused too much on how it looks and not enough on what it does? Is it heavy on graphics, but low on functionality and substance? For all its multisensory capabilities, above and beyond that, a website is a tool—a utility that people use for a specific purpose, whether it's to learn something or to buy something. Think of other utilitarian objects, like vacuum cleaners and cars. Yes, these items can and should be aesthetically pleasing—to a point. But if they're so design-heavy that they're too clunky to use, or even if they just seem to be inaccessible, they do not serve the practical purpose for which they are intended. Websites are meant to be used, not just observed.

A few years ago, there was a heated debate in web usability circles about whether graphic design was simply art that provided no tangible benefit other than making a site look better. At the pinnacle of this debate came the quick and sudden death of the online clothing store Boo.com, which had beautiful, rich graphics but absolutely lousy functionality. Although choosing the images and colors on your website and putting these visuals together in a harmonious way do play an important role in attracting and pleasing users, the functionality of your site is at least as important, and probably more important. No matter how pretty your site may be, if users cannot navigate it easily and cannot get what they came there for quickly and painlessly, the design is seriously flawed.

Always focus on the structure and content (words) of your site first, and then use good graphic design to present it in an appealing and distinctive way.

## Excessive Download Time

How long does it take for your site to come up when the user clicks on the URL or for a page to load when they click on a button on your site? If your files are too big and/or your images are not properly optimized for the web, the answer to that crucial question is: too long. A prolonged download time gives the user just enough time—and a good reason—to decide to go somewhere else.

Worse, an overloaded page can cause the user's computer to crash, guaranteeing that user will never return to your site and will be hopping mad, especially if the system failure causes the user to lose work. In terms of user experience, this is the kiss of death. Users need only one such negative experience with your site to make them superstitious about it.

Fortunately, the fix for this problem is simple: Make sure all of your images are small and take less than five seconds to load. A web images program like Adobe Fireworks or ImageReady (www.adobe.com) will give you the tools you need to create web-friendly files. Try the free trial of these programs and see which one you prefer, or use a program like Adobe Photoshop to make all of the images smaller, and then put them back where they were before on the site.

## Mistake-Riddled Content

Poor grammar, improper punctuation, misspelled words, and broken links reflect poorly, both on the quality of your site and on the professionalism of your business. These seemingly simple errors and typos can give the impression of across-the-board carelessness and neglect, as though no one is taking care of business and looking after details. It is not a long stretch for users to then wonder whether you run your whole business in a haphazard way, which might make them hesitant to order from you or to complete transactions on your site.

Most large and well-established online enterprises make a concerted effort to minimize these types of errors on their websites, and they often employ professionals whose job it is to find and fix these mistakes, preferably before the page goes live. Until and unless your business grows large enough to warrant hiring a professional to troubleshoot and maintain your website, make sure to do a thorough job of it yourself. If your spelling and grammar are awful, just find a friend or business associate to give your site the once-over for glaring errors. (My personal pet peeve is the use of "your" instead of "you're." It doesn't matter what the site is selling—for some reason, once I see this error, it's all over.)

Don't risk losing users over easy-to-remedy mistakes. Paying attention to these seemingly small details will improve the quality of your users' experience and bring long-term benefits to your business.

## Outdated Content

If you have a piece of JavaScript on your site that automatically updates the date on a certain page (some people put this on the homepage for a more personal immediate touch), this is fine. However, if you put the date in manually and don't think you can continue to do this every single day, then leave it off. This also goes for "last updated" dates, dated blog entries, and any other content that includes a date or a reference to time. For example, if the text on your site refers to a specific season of the year or to a future event that will be past tense at some point, make sure to update your site to remove or revise that text before it's old news.

If users can tell that the content isn't fresh, they're probably going to leave. Remember, simpler is better; whenever possible, avoid using dates and time-dependent content on your site.

## *Franken-Site*

Remember in the movie *Frankenstein* when the mad doctor took body parts from a bunch of dead people, sewed them together, animated them, and made a monster? Well, if you took a simple website, and then added a shopping cart, and then added a new section that doesn't quite look like the others, and then changed the graphics a little, and then added a couple of extra navigation sections because you couldn't figure out where to put them, before long you would probably have created what my colleagues and I used to call a "Franken-site."

Users can tell when a site has been patched together piecemeal, with no eye toward a cohesive structure, and they're apt to judge it to be disorganized. If they think a site is disorganized, they'll likely assume it's also difficult to use . . . and go elsewhere.

If your site has gotten to that point, it means it has outgrown your original concept—which is a natural product of growth, and so isn't necessarily a bad thing. But once you've reached the Franken-site stage, it's time to stop flogging the monster and start over. You need to totally reorganize your content, design, and architecture. Luckily, that whole process starts with the next chapter, when we will evaluate several of the top sites on the Internet.

# REAL LIFE >>
## *What Does Bob Need to Fix?*

AFTER DOING AN emergency triage of Bob's website, I diagnosed several of the problems described above. Some of these can be fixed easily and quickly, and I'll get to those in a minute. Some of the problems require more involved remedies; I've identified these, too, but will discuss them at greater length in later chapters.

### Rx for Minor Site Flaws
Resolving the following problems now will make Bob's users happier and hopefully increase his conversion rate and average visit time:

**Unrelated advertisements.** Some of the banner ads on Bob's site were added as a favor to one of his friends and have little or nothing to do with Bob's business or clientele. These oddball ads give the impression that this is not a serious business site. Advertisements for products that clearly cater to a different audience detract from the focus of the site and diminish its power as a marketing strategy. It is vitally important to define your primary user audience, and then to stick with a web strategy that focuses on that target market. Don't compromise the integrity and effectiveness of your site for friends, family, colleagues, or even potential business partners. Build a good site that is appropriate for your products, business, and clientele, and then appropriate business partners will find you.

**Slow-going.** The site takes a long time to load, which is the result of the site's images not being optimized for the web. Simply importing the main images into a program like Adobe ImageReady or Fireworks and clicking "Save for Web," then putting the smaller images back on your site will drastically decrease the load time. We'll go further into this in Chapter 10.

**Broken links.** These should either be removed completely or replaced with new links that work. Usability guru Jakob Nielsen refers to this phenomenon as "link rot" and cites it as one of the quickest ways to alienate users.

**Copy errors.** All of the grammatical, spelling, and punctuation mistakes and typos should be fixed immediately. They give the impression of a lack of professionalism and attention to detail.

**Jam-packed homepage.** Cramming a bunch of miscellaneous stuff all over the homepage makes Bob's business look disorganized and unprofessional. If the site doesn't have a clear focus and purpose, how can the user know what the site offers and how to get it? I suggest taking off about 30 percent of the homepage's elements right away, to make it look cleaner and easier to navigate. Later, we will put them back under more appropriate sections.

**No way to sign up.** I encourage Bob to immediately gather up all his customer contacts and put them into a service like Constant Contact or GetResponse. He chooses the free trial of GetResponse and immediately starts entering the list of email addresses he's gotten from the sign-up sheet at his store. He's already got 250 people who want updates, newsletters, and product information, and he needs to start reaching out to them ASAP. We'll add the simple "Sign Up" box that GetResponse provides to his site, to make sure visitors have the opportunity to sign up for more information.

Bob's site (shown below) looks much better after we correct these issues. Even with a few minor changes, Bob's site looks much less busy and more put together.

By Get Creative, Inc.

## Recovery Plan for Larger Issues

These are things we'll address in upcoming chapters:

**Lack of keywords.** Bob's website doesn't have enough keywords, period. Putting keywords in content and links would make the site a lot more search engine–friendly. Luckily, Bob did an awesome job of building a great keyword list back in Chapter 3, so going forward, it will be no problem for him to write new content that incorporates these "magnetic" words. I already gave Bob a hard time about this, though, so he's ready to make some changes and write some new articles that contain his keywords, which is the first step to search engine domination.

**Bad information architecture.** Many of Bob's top products are buried beneath a bad site structure. Where are the Amazing HomeMade Biscuits? The expert articles? Who cares about dog trivia when it's not clear how to order a simple bag of dog food? Also, this site contains one of my all-time pet peeves: quick links, which are those little links on the homepage that go directly into the content. Frankly, if you have to use quick links or anything like them, you need to reorganize your site. Direct linking like this is lazy, creates clutter, and indicates that you have more work to do on your site structure. Users should be able to easily figure out where things are just by looking at your homepage.

**Color scheme.** Prolonged exposure to white letters on a dark background creates eyestrain, making users less likely to spend much time on Bob's site. The standard black text on a white background has been proven to keep users on a site much longer.

**Inadequate content.** Because I've talked with Bob and visited his store, I know that he is a dog expert and has a wealth of information to share with customers. But there is no way for visitors to Bob's website to know that. If they did—if Bob posted his articles and cited his expertise on the site—it would position him as an authority in his field . . . and boost the site's rank in the search engines.

That's it for Parts 1 and 2. By now, hopefully you've learned some good stuff about your own site, have some great ideas, and are ready to launch into the "next phase"—building from the ground up. If you're just beginning to get your head around some of the larger concepts, that's great. Nothing to fear here.

And now . . . onward and upward!

# (Re)Design and (Re)Development

**Y**ou've taken the time to do your research and discovery. You've built your keyword list, gotten some new ideas, targeted your exact users and written about their preferences. You've calculated your current conversion rate, measured the amount of traffic going to your site, and even conducted various usability tests and focus groups to determine how people in the world are reacting to your site. You've even fixed one or two of the major problems with your current site so that it's working better already.

Armed with all of this information, you probably already have some great ideas about the direction you want your site to go. Now, in the rebuilding phase, we'll take what you already have and add the important elements of information architecture, writing, and good design. We'll talk about what you should put on the homepage, what color your links should be, how to use your keywords, and all that good stuff. So roll up your sleeves. It's time to get in there and start making some changes!

# 8 | Nail Your Site's Structure

Building a site with good bones gives users a superior online experience . . . and you a competitive advantage.

**B**y now, I'm sure you have at least some ideas about how you want your new site to look and feel, and about the killer content you're going to write for it. Before all that, though, we need to pour the foundation, so that your site is strong from the ground up. The first thing we're going to discuss in relation to your site's redesign is its structure, otherwise known as information architecture. What this really boils down to is this question: Is your site organized in the clearest way possible? During your user testing (from Chapter 6), if anyone said "I'm confused," or "I don't know where to find X," then this chapter is going to really help you reorganize your content so that it's easier for people to find, which is the first (and some say, the most important) part of a good website.

Never underestimate the value of good architecture. Just as people want a house with clean lines, a livable floor plan, and a solid foundation, your users want a site that has a smart, efficient, and reliable structure. They want (and expect) to be able to identify and access the different pieces of information on your site—seamlessly, without a glitch, and intuitively, without having to think about it. If they can't quickly and easily navigate your site, they'll click over to a competitor's site faster than they can say, "I'm outta here!" Even when they do hang in there long enough to take a look around (which in Internet Land amounts to maybe two minutes), if users can't find what they're looking for—or what *you* want them to find that they didn't even know *to* look for—you lose business. To browse means to skim through an aggregate of things looking for a specific thing. On the web, that happens very quickly and with virtually zero tolerance for delays, roadblocks, and hiccups. Given the importance of website architecture, it is amazing how little attention most people pay to it when designing their sites. People tend to focus on *what* they want to put on their websites and not to think much about *how to organize* all that stuff.

Think of it this way: If you went to your local bookstore and you couldn't find a helpful worker to ask where something was, where would you look for a copy of the children's book *Goodnight Moon*? Let's assume you know that *Goodnight Moon* is a picture book for young children written by Margaret Wise Brown. Because the store is laid out in sections, each containing a different category of book (adult fiction, biography/memoir, history, cooking, etc.), all of which are clearly marked with signs, you know to first go to the main section reserved for children's books. From there, you would go to the subsection where picture books for preschoolers were shelved, and then browse the books whose authors' last names begin with B. As another option, let's say that you'd read a book review on a parenting website, where you learned that *Goodnight Moon* is a Caldecott winner and one of the bestselling children's books of all time. In that case, you might look around for an end cap or special display where best sellers and award winners were stocked. As a third option, if the only thing you knew about the book was its title, you might do a computer search using the bookstore's online inventory system, which would list the title, author, publication date, publisher, price, and a short description of the book fitting your search criteria, as well as whether the book was in stock and in which section of the store it was shelved.

The point is: The location of each book in a bookstore is predetermined based on a hierarchical structure. On a website having content similar to that of the brick-and-mortar bookstore example, the path leading to *Goodnight Moon* might look like this:

Home > Books > Children's Books > Authors A-L > Margaret Wise Brown > *Goodnight Moon*

Now, imagine what would happen if you went to the bookstore and the books were shelved all willy-nilly, in no logical order—or at least not in an order anybody who walked in off the street could figure out? What if the books were not organized by main subjects and subtopics? What if the sections were not clearly marked? What if there was no children's section, or within the children's section there was no organizational structure? What if you could find no directory that spelled out what to find where? How much time would you spend wandering around in circles before you got frustrated and left, empty-handed and fit to be tied?

The same goes for websites. If content is strewn all over the place and/or hidden in inaccessible places on your site, it might as well not be there at all. When people encounter a disorganized or poorly organized site, they typically (and quickly) come to one or more of these damaging conclusions:

▶ Finding stuff on this site is more trouble than it's worth.
▶ This site doesn't have what I'm looking for.
▶ I'm so confused I can't remember why I even came to this site.
▶ If this muddled website is any indication of how they run their company, I'm better off taking my business elsewhere.

Usability guru and expert information architect Jakob Nielsen claims that when users get confused on your website, they tend to blame themselves, feeling stupid because they can't figure out how to use your site, and then they leave. I've found this to be true, and in my experience, bad information architecture is one of the top reasons users leave a website and never come back—right up there with bad design choices, like blurry images, ugly fonts, or garish colors. Your users should be able to glance at the navigational buckets into which you've placed your content and get a good idea of what they'll find in each. As they move around your site, they should never feel lost—no matter where they are. Please (please!) don't rely on internal search functionality to save you. Unless you're Amazon or eBay, you don't need an internal search engine to help people locate specific things on your site. You need good organization.

# The Martha Stewart of Online Organization

About.com is one of the best organized websites on the Internet. Not surprisingly, given their huge volume of information and users (tens of thousands of topics organized into "channels" and 60 million monthly visitors), About.com has a staff of information architects that are devoted to organizing the site's content.

I recommend spending a few minutes on this site, to help you get the hang of how they organize information into hierarchies. Just go to About.com (www.about.com) and click on the main subject category (channel) most closely associated with the topic you are investigating. Then follow the path leading to the information you seek.

Say, for example, that you want to find out more about Austin, Texas, where you're going next month to visit your cousin. Starting from the About.com homepage, you'd type in "Austin." From there, you'd choose "Things to Do" from the further sub-menu. On that page: Voilà! Everything you were looking for—everything from local art exhibits, to bars and restaurants on 6th Street.

Here is what that information path would look like:

Search (Austin) > Austin, TX > Things to Do

Another way to get there is to choose "Cities and Towns" from the "Browse Channels" menu on the homepage, then choose "Austin," then "Things to Do." That information pathway would look like this:

Home > Cities and Towns > Austin > Things to Do

Now, granted, About.com has more content than you would ever want or need, but you must admit they do a great job of taking a mammoth amount of information and making it simple to find what you want. Go ahead—pick a topic (any topic), go to About.com, and see how long it takes you to find what you want. About.com is always on my "favorites" list when it comes to great organization, simply because they make it look so easy.

# The A-B-Cs and 1-2-3s of Information Architecture

The key to good information architecture is organizing your content into unique categories that are specific enough to guide users to information but not so specific that they limit your ability to add content to the site. The location of each piece of content on your site—every article, every picture, every product description, and so forth—and the navigational path leading to it need to be so intuitive that the structure makes perfect sense to your users.

Each content category should be both (a) definable—meaning, you can clearly identify its contents with a one- or two-word label, and (b) scalable—meaning, you can add content to it later. For example, if you own an electronics store, designating a section on your website for "Laptops" is fine, as long as laptops are the only topic you ever talk about and/or the only product type you ever feature in that section. Once you call this section "Laptops," adding desktop computers or headphones to the section would be out of the question, because it would be the same as burying them in your backyard. No one is going to look for (or find) them there.

A smarter architecture for your electronics site might be to have a main bucket for "Computers," under which you can designate a sub-bucket for "Laptops" now, and add sub-buckets for "Desktops" and "Accessories" (to include headphones, computer speakers, printer cables, keyboards, etc.) later. Other main buckets for this site might be "Stereos," "Games," "Phones," "Software," and "Cameras."

Really, creating a strong architecture for a site is usually just a matter of common sense. Remember the outlines you had to create for term papers in high school or college? Well, organizing your website content is something like that—determining the topics in your main level of information and then the subordinate topics under each main topic.

Creating an organizational structure for your website involves these easy steps:

1. Inventory all of the content you now have (or will start with, if you don't have a site yet).
2. Brainstorm any content you might want to add in the future.
3. Sort the individual pieces of content into different categories, or buckets, grouping together items that are somehow related. Think of your website as a basket of laundry that you are sorting into "like" piles, such as bright colors, delicates, towels, and kids' play clothes.
4. Create a tab name for each bucket of content on your site. Your naming scheme should fit your business, the overall design of your site, and your target market, and each label should make sense to users and be easy for them to understand. Avoid names that are too obscure or cutesy, such as made-up words and rhyming schemes. Five years ago, using clever tab names was acceptable and (sometimes) entertaining. Today, there is so much competition on the Internet that you need to engage users right away. If they don't immediately grasp your site's nomenclature, you risk annoying and confusing them. Catchy tabs are fine and can even help to distinguish your site—but only if users can glance at them and instantly identify the gist of the content. Otherwise, you're apt to lose them in less time than it might take them to figure out that the "Ring It Up" button is actually your shopping cart.
5. To decide what goes where in your site, picture your site as a physical store, dividing it up into logical sections (like aisles or departments of the store would be), and then sort each product into its logical subsection. If you don't sell anything, then picture your site as a house, or a pile of laundry, or whatever image helps you the most. Go through each page on your site now or take a look at each product, and start deciding what subsection it logically fits into. If you get more than ten things in one section, you'll want to break it into two smaller sections, and so on. As in the About.com example, you can have an unlimited amount of content, as long as you have a strong organizational structure for it all.

# Organize Your Content

Whether you have a site already or are making one for the first time, I recommend doing a content inventory, so that you'll know what you have, what you need, and where it's all going. If you are reorganizing an existing site, you really need to take all of the content out of its current structure to see how to improve on the way it is organized.

To inventory and organize (or reorganize) your content, just follow these steps:

1. **Sort by content type.** Determine whether each piece of content that is currently on your site and/or that you intend to put on your site is an article, picture, or product description. At this point, don't worry about where on the site the item was or should be. In order to determine how to improve a site's architecture, you will need to take a fresh look at each piece of content, this time with your "ideal user/target audience" in mind. Now that you know who you're catering to, what do you think they'd be looking for first? How does the site need to be organized in order to be as clear and intuitive to them as possible? As you inventory your existing and planned content, you'll probably also think of other items you need or would like to have on your site. If you do, just make a list of content to be added.

2. **Sort by main categories.** Next, group individual pieces of content into different subjects. Try to group by main theme only for now. Though you will inevitably identify potential sub-themes during this step, just make a note of them and focus on narrowing down your main themes. These are the main buckets that will make up your site—that is, the main sections that users will see when they first go there, on the homepage. Shoot for a minimum of four main categories and no more than six or seven; otherwise you'll end up with an imbalance of content, with some sections having too little and others having too much. You'll probably need to regroup the content a few times, trying different schemes and

combinations, before you find a set of main categories that covers all the necessary first-level themes and that ensures all of the content is evenly distributed. Again, this exercise might reveal content you don't have but need; in that case, just decide which main category (or bucket) it's going in and then put it on the content wish list.

3. **Sort by subcategories.** Group the items within each main section into different sub-themes. This process usually involves re-sorting content by main theme and sub-theme, often several times, moving individual items from one section to another. Eventually, you will see a natural hierarchy—a logical order of main themes and subordinate themes—taking shape. Jot down any ideas for new content that come to you during all this sorting and re-sorting, making sure to note which bucket the content will go in.

4. **Review and revise your hierarchy.** Before you start to rebuild (or build) your site, you'll want to be sure every piece of content is in its most logical and user-friendly position. Now is the time to carefully analyze your site's structure and to move items around and re-categorize sections and subsections, as needed, until you are satisfied with the way in which all of your content is organized. Make sure you have a fairly even balance of content (number of items) under each of the top-level (horizontal) categories and each of the lower-level (vertical) subcategories. Of course, not all sections will have equal amounts of content. For example, the "Contact" and "About" sections will likely have fewer items than the sections designated for each product line and for articles. But any sections that are similar in nature should have about the same amount of content in them. For example, if you have two items in one product section but twenty in another, chances are your content is out of balance. When that happens, you'll need to do more re-grouping, renaming, and/or creating new buckets, and then redistribute your content until there is a more even distribution of content among similar buckets.

## Sample Site Structures

Here are a few examples of site structures:

**EXAMPLE A**

| Category 1 | Category 2 | Category 3 | Category 4 | Category 5 |
| --- | --- | --- | --- | --- |
| Sub 1 | Sub 2 | Sub 3 | Sub 4 | Sub 5 |
| Sub 1 | Sub 2 | Sub 3 | Sub 4 | Sub 5 |
| Sub 1 | | Sub 3 | Sub 4 | |
| Sub 1 | | | | |

This site architecture is ideal, containing enough sections in the horizontal structure to offer users adequate initial choices and at least two subcategories under each category.

**EXAMPLE B**

| Category 1 | Category 2 | Category 3 |
| --- | --- | --- |
| Sub 1 | Sub 2 | Sub 3 |
| Sub 1 | Sub 2 | Sub 3 |
| Sub 1 | | Sub 3 |
| Sub 1 | | Sub 3 |
| Sub 1 | | Sub 3 |
| | | Sub 3 |

This structure is too narrow and the content is out of balance. Category 3 has too many subcategories, thereby providing too much choice for the potential customer. This structure should be further broken up to more closely resemble Example A, above.

**EXAMPLE C**

| Category 1 | Category 2 | Category 3 | Category 4 | Category 5 | Category 6 |
| --- | --- | --- | --- | --- | --- |
| Sub 1 | Sub 2 | Sub 3 | Sub 4 | Sub 5 | Sub 6 |
| Sub 1 | | Sub 3 | Sub 4 | Sub 5 | |
| Sub 1 | | | Sub 4 | | |

This site structure is too broad. Chances are, the content under categories 2 and 6 is similar enough to content in other categories to be integrated into those other buckets, thereby creating a more balanced architecture, like the one in Example A.

Generally speaking, it is best to have about the same number of subsections under each main navigational bucket. If you go over five subsections, it's time to think about adding a new top-level section (main bucket).

Here is a great way to check the balance of content across your main sections and within each subsection:

▶ Take out your list from page 105, and write each (proposed) section name on its own note card. Also, make a note card for every piece of content on your list (or for general subcategories, if you have a huge amount of content).

▶ Use thumbtacks or tape to stick the note cards to the wall or to a bulletin board, in the order they appear within the hierarchy. For example, put all the level-one note cards in the top row, spaced far enough apart that you can put all the corresponding subsection note cards underneath each main section. This will look like a flow chart, but without the lines connecting the boxes.

▶ Check the balance of your content. Is it heavy in one section and skimpy in another? Do you need to reorganize the content to even it out? If so, start moving the note cards around until you have achieved balance and symmetry between all of the pieces of content, as in Example A. I've found that it sometimes helps to actually move the elements around until you achieve a balance.

▶ Through trial and error—by sorting and naming and by re-sorting and renaming—you will arrive at an organizational structure, or architecture, for your website that is clear, balanced, and scalable.

\* \* \*

# Expanding Your Architecture

There are times when even the best-designed websites need to be reorganized. As time goes by and your product line evolves, you add new products and discontinue others, and eventually your old buckets no longer fit the bill.

Here's an example: You have a site that sells kids' clothing. This site has a good number of repeat visitors; you and your users are happy with the way the site works; and you get a decent amount of traffic. You've got an opt-in mailing list and are communicating regularly with a growing list of customers and potential customers. Lately, you've noticed that a lot of people are asking for maternity-related stuff. Since you have the industry contacts and know where to get maternity clothing, you figure "Why not?" and add a few maternity-related sections to your site. The challenge is this: Though some people who shop for children's clothing online also shop for maternity clothes, they aren't likely to go to a children's clothing site to look for maternity clothing (or vice versa). Yes, the two industries share some customers some of the time, but they are, in fact, two separate industries with two different target markets. You want to make sure you can expand your online business without detracting from your overall brand, so that when someone comes to KidsClothing .com they don't think they're in the wrong place.

The problem with adding more stuff that's only peripherally related is that it starts to really dilute the targeted part of your targeted marketing. People are pretty specific when it comes to shopping online, and one way you can really take advantage of this is to stick almost religiously to your topic, to your target audience, and to your products. Diluting your message and your material can cost you more users than it brings in.

You've got to be really careful not to overload either of your potential markets with stuff that doesn't apply to them. If your homepage and too much of your site is filled with pregnancy pops, maternity jeans, and copies of *What to Expect When You're Expecting*, you could alienate and lose your children's clothing customers. On the other hand, if 95 percent of your homepage and too much of your site is related to kids clothing and has little or no appeal to expectant mothers, you've put off that market. The solution: either (a) structure your site to fit your first targeted market, or (b) restructure your site to suit each of your different markets, or (c) create two sister sites, each devoted to its respective product line and target market.

With small business websites, nine times out of ten it is better to stick with one or two primary users and to master that niche and develop that user base. Expanding too fast or trying to please too many different users has been the major cause of the messes I've seen with online businesses.

Now, I'm not saying don't expand. If your site is structured well, it can handle a lot of new content before it needs to be redesigned. However, it's one thing to add content that's going to be useful for your users and another thing altogether to try to get them to embrace a whole new subject, even if it might seem to you like a natural fit. If you started a site that sells handmade soap and then start marketing handcrafted furniture on the same site, it will just make you look unfocused. A better strategy would be to launch a small sub-site that's targeted to people interested in handcrafted furniture and refer them over there, or least make sure that furniture has its own section and doesn't permeate your handmade soap message.

To go back to the original example, if you are the person who owns KidsClothing.com and you want to expand into maternity wear, it's fine to make a "Maternity" section and add it to the regular structure of the site, as it's entirely possible your target audience (people shopping for kids' clothing) will also include people who are expecting a child (or know someone who is). Just be sure not to put too many maternity wear elements on the homepage, or you really will start to detract from the overall mission and scatter your audience's attention. I'd say if you find maternity wear is a great business for you and you have much more content than will comfortably fit in one section, then you should launch a "sister site" for maternity wear, with similar branding to the original site. That way you can expand the maternity wear business infinitely without disrupting the kids' clothing site.

\* \* \*

# REAL LIFE >>
## *Bob Organizes His Content*

ONE OF THE main comments from the usability testing of Bob's site was that, with the current architecture, users have no way of even knowing about the wealth of valuable information on the site in the form of articles, recipes, and anecdotes based on Bob's experiences. Because Bob has a lot of knowledge to share and because sharing this expertise can really make his site competitive, I recommend adding a section called "Knowledge" that can encompass the content Bob has now as well as anything he might come up with in the future. Bob's old information architecture:

Locations      Products      Hours      Customers      Fun Stuff

In my opinion, "Locations" and "Hours" both refer to his physical stores, and this could make him seem too small potatoes to really draw a strong online customer base. I'd recommend combining these into one category called Our Story, where he can put the locations, hours, maps, and a little story of how he started the business and how it expanded. The "Customers" section is a database of photos and stories about dogs and their owners, and there are some great ways to use those to make his site more interactive and engaging, which we'll get to a little later.

Bob's new information architecture (which we will put into effect when we redesign):

Our Story      Bob's Blog      Friends      Knowledge      Shop

This new structure will allow Bob to post new stuff on the site frequently without having to add it directly to the homepage. Bob is excited that he finally has a place for the "How to Housebreak Your Puppy" brochure.

This new structure also gives Bob the room to grow the site. If one category becomes too heavy, he can still expand, both vertically and horizontally. For now, Bob feels good about this structure, and his users will too.

# 9

# Write Killer Content

Annihilate the competition with words that pack a punch.

**C**hances are, once your site is organized into easy-to-find sections, your mind will start brimming with ideas on everything from user-appropriate design to keyword-rich copy. Now is the time to take that energy and use it to create (or re-create) some of your site's content.

The written content of a website is commonly referred to as *copy*, a term lifted straight from marketing—which makes sense, when you consider that every word on your site does, indeed, convey your marketing message. For that reason alone, the process of evaluating your site's existing copy and/or developing new copy for your site is cause for another exercise in getting real. In other words: Are you really saying what you need to say, and only what you need to say, in the way you need to say it? Is the language appropriate for your audience and for your brand? Is the writing clear, engaging, and grammatically correct? Have you given enough information, too much information, the wrong information? Bad writing is like a bad apple. A little can spoil the whole lot by failing to effectively deliver your intended message and tarnishing the user's overall impression of your site and, by extension, your business. Regardless of whether the writing flaw is something as subjective as word choice, tone, accuracy, clarity, or cohesion, or as fundamental as grammar, spelling, and punctuation, the damage inflicted by faulty or off-target writing can be fatal.

On the flip side, good writing can do wonders for your site—attracting and engaging users and enticing them to do exactly what you want them to do. When you are writing, rewriting, or selecting written content for your site, keep in mind that the key objectives of the words on your site are to:

▸ Speak directly, clearly, and compellingly to your target market
▸ Provide the information users want to know
▸ Deliver the information you want to communicate
▸ Consistently and favorably convey your brand's image
▸ Gain and sustain the interest of users
▸ Entice users to buy your products
▸ Make users feel welcome at your site, comfortable using your site, and enthusiastic about returning to your site

## What to Put on the Site

In my experience, everyone's site can benefit from engaging, well-written pieces of content. These can come in the form of blog posts, captions for a certain product, articles, or just copy you have on your homepage. The more great, original information you provide on your subject, the more people are going to find you and become your customers. This is great news for you. Chances are you have a real interest in your subject, or you wouldn't have committed your time and attention to a business (and a website) dedicated to it. So share more of the knowledge you already have! Give users a reason to come to your site.

Here's an example: A couple of years ago I did some consulting for a woman who sold jewelry made out of semiprecious stones. Her site was actually in decent shape—set up well, with products prominently displayed, and none of the obvious problems like bad information architecture, terrible design, or typos. She'd done everything right—so why was no one coming to her site, and why weren't her sales better?

The main problem I found with her site was that it lacked engaging content. Sure, the jewelry was great looking, but people need a little more information (and reason to hang out on your site) before they make a purchase. This is especially true of higher-end items. Lack of content (in the form of articles, blog posts, interesting captions, or really, anything else) also meant that this woman didn't have many keywords on her site working to her advantage with the search engines. In short, her site was just sitting there like a bump on a log, and when the occasional person did happen to find it, that person wasn't staying long enough to actually make a purchase.

Luckily, it only took one conversation with her to discover that this woman was not only a jewelry-maker, but also an expert in semiprecious stones: their meanings, history, and health-promoting properties. She even had charts and articles all about this subject, but none of this information was on her site. I suggested that she immediately make a "Knowledge" section, and post every single piece of this valuable reference information there for the world to see. This would insure that (a) people would find her site, (b) they would stay on it long enough to actually want to buy something, and (c) they would find her expertise so engaging that they would come back to see what else she had to say.

This story has a happy ending. The woman in question took my advice, put up a bunch of well-written, engaging articles about the healing properties of semiprecious stones, and within a month, her sales went up 400 percent. Needless to say, she was happy—she'd had that information in her head the whole time anyway!

So what's going to be your "magic bullet"? Generally speaking, anything that adds value to the life of your user is going to go over well. It's up to you to choose what is going to work best for yourself and your users. If you have a site up already, you probably already have a good idea of what's working and what's not. If you don't, I would recommend revisiting your site stats (Chapter 5) and seeing which parts of your site are the most frequently visited. That is what your users are responding to, so it is best to focus your attention on giving them more of what they want. For instance, if you put up an article that gets a ton of good feedback and/or page views, look back at that article to see why it worked. Was it broken into bite-size chunks? Was the subject matter particularly engaging? Sometimes a unique angle on a subject you know like the back of your hand is all you need to start an article series that people will love and refer to for years to come. Sometimes adding a simple blog to your site can be just the attractor it needed.

# Write Keyword-Rich Content

Here's where we get out your keyword list (from Chapter 3) and start putting it to use. Take a look at that list now.

From now on, when writing content for your site (or having others write it), make sure that content contains these keywords. By actually writing the keywords into the content, you are making sure the search engines will find you, while you keep your content focused on the overall theme of your site. If you find it difficult to fit the keywords into already existing content for the site, try writing some new articles that focus on one or two keywords. Since you need to be adding new content on a regular basis anyway, do this exercise frequently.

I don't want to put too much emphasis on the importance of keyword-rich content/articles on your site because, of course, you have to write about what interests you or it's going to be tough to keep doing it. But all things being equal, keyword-rich content does make a big difference when you're trying to get to the top of the search engine results. So if you're like the lady in the example above (the expert in semiprecious stones), you already have the knowledge—you just need to put it into the form that's going to help you the most when it comes to the search engines. The way to do this is just to be sure to have your keyword list in front of you when you're writing the content for your site. You'll be surprised at what a difference it makes, not only in the ideas that it gives you, but in how your traffic starts to go up after you implement this strategy. People want to know what you know. It's just a matter of connecting you with them.

It does take some practice to integrate the keywords into your site without sounding like a robot. Once you're done reworking your content, you might want to test the site's overall "keyword density" by visiting one of these sites (they're both free): www.keyworddensity.com or www.webjectives.com/keyword.htm.

# Web Writing Guidelines

As important as it is to say the right thing on your site (and not to say the wrong thing), it is also important not to say too little or too much. Of all these potential writing faux pas, copy overkill (too many words) is hands-down the most common, affecting 90 percent of all the sites out there today. So what about your site? Do you have the burden of too many words? Why, you might ask, is this even a problem?

Here's something no one ever tells you: People don't read on the web. They scan. That is why, when developing content for your site, you'll need to get to your point quickly, state it succinctly, and not waste words on superfluous detail. Here are some general guidelines for developing web content:

**Keep it above the fold.** As a rule of thumb, all of the vital content on a page should be visible without having to scroll down. The bulk of your content and any action items (for example, newsletter sign-up or a "Buy" button) should always appear above the fold (the one-page mark). This doesn't mean you have to just have a site that fits into a one-screen section. It's okay to have stuff "below the fold" as well—just make sure you have all of your navigation and some engaging content to hook them in that one screen.

**Create strong and concise headlines.** Studies show that you've got about five seconds to grab the attention of the average American. So if your headline doesn't capture the users' interest, they aren't going to read the content that follows. Writing great headlines, taglines, and photo captions is more art than science. Some people come by it naturally; others do well enough with plenty of practice. If you're in doubt, you can always call in a professional (see page 123).

**Write short, simple sentences.** Try to limit the length of most sentences to about ten words. Don't sacrifice clarity or quality for the sake of brevity, though. Be as brief *and* as clear as possible. Avoid compound and run-on sentences, unnecessary adjectives and adverbs (descriptive words), and excessive punctuation, such as too many commas, colons, or dashes.

**Avoid long paragraphs.** Nothing is more intimidating and off-putting to a user than long blocks of dense text. Break your copy into paragraphs of no more than ten lines (or so) and use a blank line (rather than an indented first line) to separate paragraphs. Definitely consider breaking an article or subject into bullet points for easier understanding.

**Imbed keywords . . . judiciously.** Try to include keywords (see Chapter 3) in your content, but do it sparingly and make sure they fit seamlessly into the message. If you load your copy with too many blatantly obvious keywords, you'll end up alienating your audience.

This cannot be overemphasized: You are writing for real people, not search engines.

**Remember the user over your shoulder.** This means always keeping your primary user in mind when developing web content; always write as though you were speaking directly to that person. Let's call her Mary. If Mary is unlikely to care about the topic you're thinking of writing about, either ditch the idea or find an angle that will be relevant to her. If an article someone asks you to post on your site contains language that might offend Mary or a concept that might bewilder her, either omit the piece or edit it to fit your primary user.

**Convey a consistent message and tone.** Your message is the underlying meaning (the gist) of what you're saying, while your tone is how (the style with which) you communicate that message. These two key elements are intrinsically linked—meaning you can't have one without the other. If the message is spot-on but the tone is off-track, the wrong tone will undermine the right message, and vice versa. When the message jibes with the tone—and when both the message and tone jibe with the target market and with your brand—that's about as good as good web copy gets. I've provided several examples on pages 121–22 of websites with good copy that caters to its audience. Apple.com also has a great standard of writing—engaging, clear, and definitely catering to their target audience of educated computer-lovers.

As far as bad copy goes, I'm generally not one to point fingers (unless they've hired me to do so). Websites can change overnight, and I don't want to embarrass someone unnecessarily who may have wised up by the time you read this. However, if some examples of bad writing would be useful to you, then you should visit the website of Vincent Flanders, whose Web Pages That Suck site does a great job of cataloging the best of the worst on the Internet. He's got many examples of terrible writing on his site (www.webpagesthatsuck.com), including one unfortunate webmaster who's used the word "darling" like it's going out of style (which, in case you're curious, it is).

**DON'T SHOUT!** Studies have shown that after the first few words, people just tune out anything that's in all caps. Besides, it's obnoxious. I AM NOT KIDDING ABOUT THIS. TYPE THAT'S IN ALL CAPS DISTRACTS USERS FROM YOUR MESSAGE. PLUS, IT MAKES YOU LOOK LIKE AN AMATEUR.

**Don't stress the small stuff.** And when it comes to putting added emphasis on web content, 99.9 percent of it is small stuff. If you want to use exclamation points, or bold, or italics to stress a point that's really important or exciting, go ahead—*emphasize!* Just use these tactics sparingly—no more than two per page and no more than a handful on the whole site. Remember, overemphasizing has the same effect as shouting with all caps: When you place special importance on too many things, users are apt to conclude that none of it is important.

**Choose an appropriate font.** When it comes to web text, size matters. If the type is too small, users will need a magnifying glass—or, God forbid, have to adjust the font preferences in their browser—to read it; too large, and it overwhelms the page. Some fonts are incompatible with certain browsers, and others might be interesting to look at but difficult to read. So resist the temptation to use fancy fonts, and instead stick with universal fonts that will work for the majority of browsers: Arial, Courier, Helvetica, Times New Roman, and Verdana.

You'll also want to be consistent in how you use varying fonts, colors, and styles (regular, bold, italic, etc.) throughout your site. Do yourself and your site a favor, and for consistency's sake, create a style sheet that specifies the font, size, color, and style of each element of your content. For example:

**Headlines: Arial, 14-point, bold, blue**
**Body Text:** Times New Roman, 11-point, black
**Excerpts:** *Times New Roman, 11-point, italic, black*
**Captions:** Arial, 10-point, blue

Your style sheet doesn't have to look like this one, but it does have to be consistent, and you should commit to using it all throughout your site. In this example, all of your captions would be in 10-point blue Arial. That's how your users will know they're looking at captions and not body copy. Set a style sheet for your site and stick to it. It's just one more step in making your site's content look consistent and professional.

**Fix your typos.** I mentioned this before in Chapter 7, but it's important enough to say again in our discussion of content in general. When you're writing new copy for your site, be sure it's not only clear and engaging, but free of errors. Spelling, punctuation, and grammatical errors and typos make your site look poorly tended, at best, and unprofessional, at worst. This is your face to the world we're talking about here. If you can't tell the difference between "you're" and "your," you are not getting my credit card information; I don't care how cool your site looks or how knowledgeable you are about your chosen subject. Here's the best analogy I've ever heard to describe this problem: "A good-looking website riddled with copy errors is like a guy in a great-looking suit with missing teeth." With that horrifying image fresh in your mind, I encourage you to go over your site with an obsessive eye or offer your most grammar-obsessed friend lunch on you in exchange for proofing your site for typos.

# Content to Write Home About

Here are two examples of well-written content that hits all the right marks:

## ESPN
*www.espn.go.com*

ESPN's target audience appears to be eighteen- to thirty-five-year-old male armchair athletes, and the website copy reflects this. Every word of content on the site is short, to the point, and filled with energy—like a sports broadcast or something you'd yell when you're watching an exciting football game. ESPN's content is tailored to sports-watching, adrenaline-pumping guys—from the headlines ("Frozen in Time," "Fighting Spirit"), to the regular copy ("Chris Burke's blast ended the longest game in playoff history . . .")—screams, "This is a site for sports lovers!"

## *Real Simple* Magazine
*www.realsimple.com*

*Real Simple*'s demographic is totally different from ESPN's, so naturally the tone of the writing on this site is much different than what would appeal to sports-loving guys. From the site's tagline, "Life made easier," to article titles, such as "12 Ways to Cut Clutter," the copy is refined and straightforward, in keeping with any matriarch of domestic harmony, and completely devoid of the hyperbolic language found throughout ESPN.com. The target audience of Real Simple is (most likely) women aged twenty-five to forty who have families and busy lives, and all of the content appeals to these women. *Real Simple* magazine strives to help make your life easier, and their website is no different; each headline is eye-catching because it's about something you could use to make your life a little better in a short period of time. That's good content!

What you can take away from these examples is simple:

▸ Make sure every aspect of your content—from the topics you write about, to the words you choose and the tone of the writing—is appropriate for your primary audience.
▸ Make sure the writing is consistent across every piece of content on your site, from the tagline and link titles to every headline, caption, and article.

Keep these things in mind when writing (or acquiring and editing) each piece of content for your site, and you will deliver the intended message to the target audience with the hoped-for results.

# Where to Find Help

Over the past ten years or so, it has become increasingly clear that good writing is essential to good website usability. That reality can be intimidating to someone who doesn't have much, if any, experience writing anything, much less something as specialized as web content. Writing copy for your site can be especially daunting if you're starting with nothing and will have to write every word from scratch.

So what do you do if you know you're not a good writer, or if writing is just not your thing? Because of the vital importance of making sure that every word on your site counts, this is one area where I really recommend getting some professional help.

If the thought of writing your site's content strikes fear into your heart, here are some options that can give you a leg up.

### Take a Class

Many colleges, universities, and trade schools offer fine copy-writing courses, and some even offer web content development classes. Your local community college probably has one you can audit.

Another option is to take an online course. If you decide to take this route, I suggest going with a course from an online university or a writer's association, rather than with a self-proclaimed copy writing expert. The HTML Writers Guild offers good courses such as "Web Content Writing and Editing." You can find these at www.hwg.org/services/classes. At the very least, start educating yourself on the do's and don'ts by visiting Useit.com (www.useit.com/papers/webwriting) and reading their guidelines for writing on the web.

With instruction, practice, and feedback from your instructor and peers, you'll begin to get the hang of copy writing.

## Hire a Professional

If you know you're not a great writer, consider hiring someone to do the first version of your site copy for you, while you're learning. Before hiring a writer for your site, always look at her or his work samples first. Go to the websites for which the writer has contributed content to see whether this person has written a decent amount of web content, accurately captured the tone, and delivered a clear message. Make sure the writer has experience writing everything from banner ads to web content to broadcast emails, and any other form of writing you think you might need. Ideally, you want to have one person who knows your site and content needs well and can write anything and everything you need. Finally, always ask for references and check them out.

Here are some ways to find professional writers:

**Word of mouth.** Start with your circle of friends and associates. If someone you know has a writer who has worked well for them, ask if that person takes on freelance assignments. Sometimes the best people are so busy that they don't have time to advertise. If you see something you think would work for your site, try to find the person who did it.

**Craigslist.** There are many excellent writers in every city, some of whom have posted their resumes on Craigslist (in the "Resumes" section). Another option is to post an ad for a website writer in the "Jobs" section. (Craigslist charges for job listings in the biggest cities.) Advertise for a website writer, and you'll get a slew of resumes and portfolios for your review. Choose a writer with a reasonable rate whose previous work you feel matches your goals for your site. Ask the writer for an estimate for the whole site, and how much it will cost to provide periodic updates.

**Online marketplaces.** An "online marketplace" is a site that posts the portfolios and resumes of many writers, sometimes from all over the world. If you can't find what you're looking for on Craigslist, you might want to open up your search by using one of them. Here's how it works: You sign up and post your project for free, and then let the talent come to you with bids. Or you can just spend some time browsing through portfolios. Posting a project is also a great way to clarify what you need, your goals for the site, and the approximate amount of work you have cut out for you. Visit www.allfreelancework.com or www.elance.com to browse around and post projects; another site specific to web content development is www.web-content-writers.com.

# Where to Find Additional Content

The thought of developing an entire library of good content for a website can be overwhelming, especially if you're not a confident writer and you're starting with next to nothing. If you're not up to the task of writing everything yourself, you can grab some free stuff to bulk up what you've already got.

## *The Public Domain*

Any piece of writing that is in the public domain is free to use—without the risk of copyright infringement. This does not mean you can take credit for something that someone else wrote (like, for example, saying you wrote *Hamlet*), but you can use quotes, excerpts, or whole articles and books that are in the public domain without having to ask permission or pay royalty fees. You should, of course, always give credit where credit is due and cite the author and the published title of whatever public domain content you post on your site. According to the U.S. Copyright Office (www.copyright.gov/pr/pdomain.html), under the current copyright laws of most countries, including the United States, a written work passes into the public domain when all of the following criteria are met:

- ▸ The work was created and first published before January 1, 1923, or at least ninety-five years before January 1 of the current year, whichever is later;
- ▸ The last surviving author [or lawful heir] died at least seventy years before January 1 of the current year;
- ▸ No Berne Convention [an international copyright agreement between cooperating nations] signatory has passed a perpetual copyright on the work; and
- ▸ Neither the United States nor the European Union has passed a copyright term extension since these conditions were last updated. (This must be a condition because the exact numbers in the other conditions depend on the state of the law at any given moment.)

Copyright laws are very complex, and they vary from country to country. Unauthorized use of copyrighted matter is a serious legal matter, and definitely not something you want to contend with. So make sure that the material you want to use is really in the public domain before you put it on your site. Your best assurance of using only legitimate public domain content on your site is to use a known provider of public domain content.

One site with a great number of public domain works is Project Gutenberg, named after Johannes Gutenberg, the man credited with printing the first book (a Bible). And you thought this book was only about websites!

Here are the URLs for three reliable sources of public domain content:

www.gutenberg.org
www.ibiblio.org
www.public-domain.org

## The Government

If you pay taxes, then technically you paid for all the reports and publications produced by the federal and state governments. If you don't pay taxes, then the rest of us taxpaying citizens are covering your share of this one.

According to Wikipedia, Title 17 USC §105, Subject Matter of Copyright: United States Government Works provides that: Copyright protection is not available for any work of the United States Government, [defined as] a work prepared by an officer or employee of the United States Government as part of that person's official duties. Therefore, only those works solely authored by U.S. federal government employees are not protected by copyright in the United States.

Every state in this country has a similar copyright waiver on any published material created solely by that state's governing body. This means you can take any content published by the federal government or any state government and reprint it, in part or in whole, on your website without asking permission and without paying royalty fees. Just make sure that the content was, indeed, produced exclusively for and by the federal or state government, and reprint it to your heart's content.

Again, it's always a good idea to include a statement on your site crediting the content's original source.

Check out www.firstgov.gov and click on "Reference" for articles, reports, photos, and graphics produced by our government for your use.

## Content Providers

These days, many websites offer a wide variety of free or low-cost articles. These include iSnare (www.isnare.com), ArticleCity (www.articlecity.com), and GoArticles (www.goarticles.com). The only catch with these articles is that they're essentially a promotion for the author's website, and you can use their content only if you provide a link on your site to their site. Also, since they're free or really cheap, anyone can use them, so some of the content on your site won't be original and could be on a gazillion other websites. Unoriginal content that links to someone else's site is certainly not the ideal, but it beats a page full of banner ads with nothing compelling to read.

### "Free" Content Guidelines

Before you post content from the public domain, the government, or any of the free article services on your site, first make sure that it:

**Fits the subject matter of your site.** Never add content merely for the sake of having more words on your site. It will only dilute the user experience you've worked so hard to build. This is another case for quality over quantity. Make sure the new content has some inherent value to your primary user.

**Matches the tone of your site.** Ensuring that any outside content that you add is consistent with the other content on your site and appropriate for your target market means not only paying attention to what is said but also to how it is said. If your primary user is a fourteen-year-old boy, he probably doesn't want to read something written in Elizabethan English.

**Is web-friendly.** Don't put a four-thousand-word article on your site, or at least not all on one page. Edit the content to slice it into bite-size portions that go with the flow of good web design.

## REAL LIFE >>
### Bob Breaks His Content Down

WHEN BOB ORIGINALLY put his site together, he didn't have the time or the inclination to actually edit the content or to go over it with a fine-tooth comb to catch and clean up copy errors. Consequently, the site still has typos, protracted sentences, awkward phrasing, and big chunks of content crowding the page. This is a good example of the "big chunks of content" problem plaguing Bob's site (see page 128).

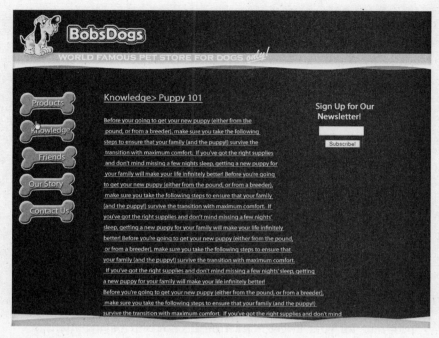

By Get Creative, Inc.

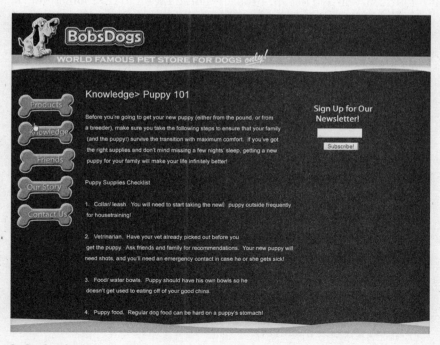

By Get Creative, Inc.

The site also features several informational brochures that Bob wrote to use as handouts at his physical store—such as "How to Care for Your Dog's Sensitive Skin," "Easy House Training for Your Puppy," and "How to Care for a Rescue Dog." Bob stuck these up on his site without editing a word, and most of these articles exceed 2,000 words and have long sentences. I suggest trimming all of these articles down to 500 to 750 words each and editing them to make sure each sentence is short, snappy, and to the point. (Try using bullets, Bob!) All of these articles will fit nicely into the "Knowledge" section we made in the last chapter.

I also encourage Bob to enlist the aid of a friend or a college student to thoroughly proofread the entire site so Bob can clean up those typos and grammar, punctuation, and spelling errors once and for all.

Just changing the format of the article and correcting the bad grammar makes this article infinitely more user-friendly (see below). Later, Bob can also add links from within the articles to his online store, allowing people to read the articles and then order products all at once.

# 10 | Design to Please

Good design means creating a look that both appeals to your target market and compliments your brand.

**N**ow that you've got your content all ready to go and have organized it appropriately, it's time to add some design into the mix, so the whole thing is pleasing to your user's eyes and is appropriate to your brand. But how much design do you need to really make your website great? The debate over how much emphasis to place on a site's graphic design (also called design) is one that seems to have been going on since the first day of the Internet. For those who are just joining this story-in-progress, here is how it's gone so far:

In the beginning, there was the Internet. Thousands and thousands of geeks wrote code all day long, putting web pages out there in cyberspace to be viewed over a vast network of technology by thousands and thousands of other geeks. For a while, people (mostly geeks) were content to create and to visit sites constructed entirely of text. Then other people discovered the World Wide Web, and soon they became more sophisticated in their online expectations. No longer was it cool for every website to look basically the same. Users wanted to be able to tell websites apart, and website owners wanted to distinguish their sites from others so users would notice them, spend more time there, and come back. Before long, both users and owners were craving variety and pizzazz. They wanted websites with more functionality, more content, more . . . design.

Hence, the job of web designer was created, and it was good.

Originally, the designer's job was to add visual elements (pictures, color, shading, borders, etc.) and symmetry (the arrangement of design elements and text on a page) to a site. The goal wasn't so much to create an artistic design as it was to effectively translate a company's brand into what was called a recognizable web presence, so that, for example, when users logged on to Sears.com, they'd know essentially what they were going to get.

So designers started laying on the graphics. Nothing wrong with that, right? Well, actually, there was a problem with that. Graphic means visual—essentially, pictures . . . period. And humans stopped communicating solely with pictures about 2 million years ago. In the modern world, which was now all about multimedia, a good web design meant not only good graphics but also good words (engaging), good organization (smooth navigation), and good function (works properly). Oh, and the entire site now needed to be strategically designed for a clearly defined target market . . . and, of course, as it was in the beginning of web graphics history, it had to effectively convey the brand.

Suddenly, "You look marvelous" didn't cut it anymore. Beautiful pictures can take you only so far, even if you're the Museum of Modern Art (which, by the way, has a fantastically organized website; check it out at www.moma.org).

The moral of this story: *Form should always follow function.*

In other words, a site's design (graphics) must always be driven by its purpose (why it exists and how it is used) and its content (what you put in it). Yes, looks are important, but only in so far as they support the main objective of attracting users to your site and providing them with a positive user experience in which they do what you want them to do there and come back to do it again.

Maybe after reading my little story about the history of web design, you're convinced that your high-concept site is design-heavy and the graphics need to be pared down and toned down. Maybe your site just needs a face-lift, a nip here and a tuck there—rearranging a few parts, updating a few pieces, smoothing out a few wrinkles—to make it look good as new. Maybe, now that you're looking at it for what it is—namely, a function- and content-driven design that needs to work well *and* look good—you realize that your site needs an extreme makeover.

If anything in the first half of this book (such as usability testing, focus groups, user feedback, the triage list, or your site stats) is telling you that your site needs a total design overhaul, please don't get discouraged.

You're not alone. Even the big guys have to continually tweak and periodically redesign their sites. Unlike a book or a film or a brochure or a CD, a website is not a static publication that you create once and it stays that way forever. A website is dynamic—meaning, it is meant to be changed. There is an immediacy to the Internet that is absent from other forms of publication, and users expect the information on a website to be current and for the site to reflect current design and market trends. The only way to stay ahead of that curve and to stay competitive online is to continually update your site. Early in the life of most websites, updates are usually limited to adding and refreshing content, and a well-designed site enables you to make those types of minor changes without having to revamp the design itself. It is only a matter of time, however, before the site's natural evolution will dictate a design face-lift or overhaul.

Whether you're making a few cosmetic changes to your site, completely renovating the design, or building a brand-new design for the first time, here are a few things to keep in mind.

## Put Your Words to Work

Why, you might ask, am I talking about content in a chapter devoted to design? Because imbedding keywords in graphic images—where search engines can't find them—is one of the most common and costly mistakes people make when designing their sites. The only words that search engines can read are the words in HTML files (text). When a search engine scans a graphics file, it sees only the image; it cannot read the words imbedded in that image. This is true of all graphics files, including images created in programs such as Adobe Photoshop or Fireworks, JPEG or GIF images, or anything dynamically generated, such as words contained in a database. Whole documents existing on your site as PDF or even Microsoft Word files also fall into this category.

Let's say that as the owner of the online kids' clothing store we talked about in an earlier chapter you have a stunning digital photo of three darling children decked out in your bestselling duds. Perfect for your homepage! Being the astute marketer you are, you write an attention-grabbing headline and a few lines of brilliant promotional copy, making sure to include a few keywords in them. Using Adobe Photoshop, you copy and paste the headline into the file containing the photo, and position it just so. Looks fantastic! And now, you've got your dazzling photo, your clever copy, and your keywords all in one file. How smart is that? Well, actually, not so smart—because it's a graphics file, and search engines can't read words in graphic files, and the keywords you so carefully positioned on the image are nowhere else on your site, and so the search engines will never ever find them.

Assuming you don't already know whether your site was made in Adobe Photoshop or another graphics program, here's how to find out whether search engines will be able to find all the words on your site:

1. Go to any page on your site.
2. Press Ctrl+U (both keys simultaneously). This will reveal the site's source code. You can also see the source code by going to "View" in your website browser, and selecting "Source" (it's usually near the bottom of the list).
3. Scroll down to view the code for the content on that page. HTML text will not appear as actual words and images, but will be represented by lines of code starting with "<img src=>."
4. What you see here is what the search engine sees when it visits your site. If you don't know what this is, not to fear—we'll get there in Chapters 14 and 15. For now, quickly skim the lines of code that appear—no need for you to actually know what any of it means. What you're looking for are the actual words that appear on your site, like "Welcome to the baby store." If what you see is just a big blank screen, that means that all of your text is imbedded in something, like frames or image files or Flash, and that the search engine is not seeing any of it. I repeat—what

you see here is what the search engine is seeing. If you see nothing, this is why people aren't finding your site.

What you're looking for are the actual words that appear on your site, such as "Welcome to the baby store." If what you see is just a blank screen, that means all of your text is embedded, like in frames or image files or Flash, and the search engine is not seeing it. What you see here is what the search engine is seeing, and if you see nothing, that is why people aren't finding your site. Search engines read code, not images. If there are any words in your site that are inside graphic files, I urge you: *Set them free!*

If a word is important enough to be on your website, it's important enough to be seen by a search engine. With the possible exception of navigation text (which we'll cover in the next chapter), you want to get credit for every word on your site. Never put words inside graphics; if you do, you are just cheating yourself out of search engine rankings.

This might mean retyping every word into new pages in an HTML-editing program like Dreamweaver, or into whatever website-building software you're using (from TypePad's templates to GoDaddy's WebSite Tonight to Intuit's Homestead). All of them will need you to build separate pages with separate words on them that can actually be seen by the search engines. If your site consists mainly (or solely) of images or Flash now, you will be shocked at the difference these new pages make in the amount of traffic you're getting to your site.

You worked hard for those words. Make sure they work hard for you.

## The Beauty of Simplicity

If you take only one thing away from this chapter, let it be this: Resist the urge to overdesign. People often try to make their websites stand out by adding fancy backgrounds, strange color combinations, avant-garde fonts, blinking graphics, and gobs of photographs, clip art, and other images. To this, I repeat: Content is king. Content is what drives traffic to your site, and content should be what drives the design of your site.

Don't hide or diminish your content with a garish design—and whatever you do, don't substitute a bunch of window dressings for good content. When a site is too busy or too intense to look at, it tends to make users feel overwhelmed and irritated. If a design is way over the top, it can be like an assault on the senses, and then the natural impulse is to look (or get) away. Going overboard with design is a good way to drive users away—so as a rule of thumb, it is best to keep the design clean and simple.

On the other hand, you don't want to go for a generic, plain-old-vanilla look either. Your design should be as interesting and distinctive as your content, and the visual tone of your site should be appealing to your target market. Creativity is good. Individuality is good. A good balance of style *and* substance is great. Just remember: An overdesigned site is an undermined site. The best designs are usually clear and compelling reflections of the core values of a brand. Stick with those, and you can't go wrong.

## Cash In on Your Brand Equity

You probably already defined your brand when you started your company and have infused it into everything you've done—from your logo to your products and marketing materials. In that case, you'll want to convey that same brand in the look and feel of your website, in order to capitalize on and to strengthen your brand recognition in the market.

If you haven't defined your brand yet, now is a good time to do it, before you design (or redesign) your website. That way, as you develop or update each aspect of your business—whether it's your website, logo, tagline, brochures, product, or lines—your brand will be reflected consistently throughout your enterprise . . . and will become instantly recognizable to customers and potential customers.

What is a brand? My dictionary defines brand as:

> A product, service, or concept that is publicly distinguished from other products, services, or concepts so that it can be easily communicated and usually marketed. A brand name is the name of the distinctive product, service, or concept. Branding is the process of creating and disseminating the brand name. Branding can be applied to the entire corporate identity as well as to individual product and service names.

Walter Landor, one of the greats of the advertising industry, says this about branding: "Simply put, a brand is a promise. By identifying and authenticating a product or service it delivers a pledge of satisfaction and quality."

Even if you haven't formally defined your brand, you probably already have a good idea of what it consists of. If you don't already have a handle on this, here's a simple exercise that will help you to define your brand.

1. Describe the essence of your business in a single phrase, keeping your target market in mind. For example:
   - An upscale store that sells designer baby clothes
   - An edgy arts and culture magazine for hip urbanites
   - A general contractor specializing in "green" building
   - An adventure travel agency catering to baby boomers
   - An online discount tool site for auto mechanics
   - A law firm specializing in malpractice cases
2. Make a list of all the attributes that you associate with your business, products (or services), and target market. Just in case you're stuck trying to come up with a list of brand attributes, here are a few popular examples:

   My brand is _____ (fill in all that apply):
   Alternative
   Artsy
   Avant-garde
   Beautiful
   Clean
   Conservative
   Edgy
   Fashionable
   Fun
   Happy
   High-End
   Hip
   Inexpensive
   Natural

Sexy
Simple
Smart
Soft
Traditional
Trendy
Trustworthy
Upbeat
Upscale Urban
Wholesome

3. On your list of attributes, identify the top five—that is, the five traits that best describe your business, distinguish it from the competition, and represent your target market. These five key themes are the essence of your brand and should be reflected throughout your enterprise, including your website's design.

4. Next, take the words you've associated with your brand and match them up with the color association list on pages 130–140. For instance, if you run a vitamins and health food site, you're probably going to want to be known as "wholesome," "healthy," and "fresh" as well as "knowledgeable" and "trustworthy." Those words and feelings would typically lend themselves to a combination of greens, possibly blues, and maybe an emphasis on white (for freshness and because white space is a great thing to use in your site, because it draws the user's eye to content you might want to highlight, makes images appear more dramatic, and gives the user's brain time to take it all in).

# Color Your World

It goes without saying, but since so many people seem to forget this when designing their websites, I'll say it anyway: When choosing colors for your site, remember the "do not overdesign" rule. Also, always keep in mind your brand—and, by extension, your primary user. Color selection presents yet another case for defining your primary user up front. When you know your users to a T, you can design for, and to please, them.

For example, if you're selling sporting goods and gear for rugged men, I suggest not choosing the pink, yellow, and blue pastels you might see on a baby furniture site. With your color choices, as with all other design elements on your site, you want to assure users that you know them and that your company exists for them. Look at your site through their eyes. What colors would you expect and like to see there if you were visiting it for the first time? What colors come to mind when you envision these people and the environment in which they might use your product or service?

Another helpful thing to do when choosing your site's colors is to go back and check out the colors (as well as the technology choices) on your Top Five Sites. Do you see any combinations that appeal to you and are appropriate for your brand and target market? Another exercise that can be helpful is to check out the colors of your five biggest competitors' sites. Since some of them probably share your target audience, what are they doing to cater to them?

Most websites have a definitive theme of at least two and no more than four different colors that are used consistently throughout the site. Choose colors from the same palette (family)—in other words, colors that go well together. That does not mean using a monochromatic color scheme in which all of the colors are simply varying shades within the same color family—unless you want to use a monochromatic color scheme and it works for your site and your users. It is perfectly fine and often advantageous to include contrasting colors in your color scheme. Just make sure all the colors complement one another—and that it's not too much.

When there are too many colors on a website, or when the colors are overly bright or discordant with one another, looking at the screen for any length of time can cause eye fatigue. It can also be a real turnoff for users. You certainly don't want your color scheme to give customers a headache or turn their stomachs. Just as it is important for your colors to go with one another, they also need to go with the rest of the content on your site, your brand, and your target market. Base your color choices on your site's primary objective—which is to attract and please users—and to that end, on the emotional response you want your design to evoke. For example, you may want to use warm shades to convey a sense of calm, bright colors to convey excitement, or rich tones to convey prestige. An effective technique to use when selecting a color scheme for your site is to lift colors from the environment in which your product or service will be used. For example, if your website is for a bed and breakfast in a scenic location, you could choose colors that figure prominently in the photographs of the area on your site. For a rustic log cabin inn in Montana, they might be forest green and cedar brown. For an adobe inn nestled in the red rocks of Sedona, Arizona, the colors might be desert beige, cayenne red, and sage green. For a beach bungalow on Maui, they might be coral, yellow, and brilliant blue.

There are many ways to approach selecting a color scheme for your website. Of course, your personal color preferences will inevitably affect your choices. That's okay. Just don't let your passion for your favorite colors overrule common sense and your business sense. Choose what you like, but make sure your color scheme fits your primary user, your brand, and the basics of good design, the most basic of which is, keep it clean and simple.

## Color Associations

For your reference, here is a list of colors and some common associations ascribed to them. For this expert analysis, I turned to lighting designer extraordinaire Tim Becker, from Fluid Lighting (www .fluidlighting.com).

Generally speaking, warm, cold, and neutral indicate that color's typical hue. White and black are considered base colors, and only acquire a hue when another color is added to them.

**Red (warm).** Red is readily visible and attracts attention. Red represents intensity and urgency; it is the color of blood, fire, heat, desire, war, danger, rage, strength, power, and speed. Some say looking at the color red can increase your blood pressure, metabolism, and appetite. Red is commonly used for stop signs, "For Sale" signs, and "Buy Now" and "Click Here" buttons. Lighter shades of red and pink might represent love, passion, and romance.

**Orange (warm).** Orange is also highly visible and quite intense but less so than red. Orange is associated with sunshine, joy, creativity, autumn, energy, and warmth. As an interesting side note, in 1999, orange was the most frequently used color on websites.

**Yellow (warm).** Yellow is associated with energy, sun, warmth, happiness, optimism, intellect, and spontaneity. Yellow can be used to complement and to highlight, but shouldn't be used extensively, because too much yellow can overwhelm. Yellow is not a good choice for text, for the obvious reason that it is difficult to read.

**Green (cool).** Green is the primary color of nature, healing, growth, prosperity, and harmony. Green is soothing and is often associated with freshness, purity, money, and recreation.

**Brown (neutral).** Brown is the color of earth, structure, and wholesomeness.

**Blue (cool).** Blue is the color of the sea and the sky. Blue is fluid, cool, receding, calming, clear, intuitive, and vocal. The color blue represents truth, intelligence, faith, heaven, confidence, vision, peace, agreement, and consciousness. Blue is at the far end of the color spectrum from red and represents the opposite of red. Dark blue is common among corporate logos and can represent depth and stability.

**Purple (warm or cool).** Purple, a mixture of red and blue, literally combines the energy and excitement of red with the depth and stability of blue. For some, this combination is psychologically difficult to resolve and can create tension, but for more people, purple represents power, luxury, mystery, magic, and rarity. The color purple is often associated with royalty, fantasy, and the artist formerly known as Prince (and now known as Prince again).

**White (base).** Technically, white is the combination of all the colors of light. In essence, a rainbow (which is simply a shaft of sunlight) is white, and its colors come from the light's reflection on water (clouds/rain). White represents purity, clarity, innocence, cleanliness, levity, light, goodness, virginity, impenetrability, godliness, faith, life, and safety. Other associations: dairy, angels, hospitals, and health.

**Black (base).** Technically, black is the absence of light and, hence, the absence of color. Black can represent power, authority, strength, elegance, and formality—or, on the other side of the fence, it can represent fear, death, despair, evil, and enigma. Black is also associated with simplicity. Black in combination with other colors can be very powerful. On a website, too much black, especially as a background or in large chunks, can distract attention and cause the images on the page to recede. The human eye is attracted to and stimulated by light. When bombarded with black, which is the absence of light, we are compelled to try to escape the darkness and to look for other visual stimuli.

Based on this list of colors and their associations, think about a color scheme for your site that is appropriate, both to your brand and to your demographic. For instance, a site that focuses on eco-friendly architecture is likely to be clean-looking and have green and white as its main color themes, while financial institutions are more likely to design with a shade of dark blue that instills trust and confidence in their visitors. I would recommend giving some thought to this, but not getting overly bogged down; while I do think that design (and keeping your target audience in mind) is very important, I have seen more sites succeed on the basis of strong, relevant content than gorgeous design. Yes, design does make an impression (and a difference) overall, but in the long run, if you're giving your users consistent quality content to read and refer back to, they're going to be less likely to care about the package it's in.

So if you've had enough of color theory and are confident about the colors you've chosen for your site, that's great. If you want to delve deeper, I would suggest looking at the very interesting blog/site Design

Melt Down (www.designmeltdown.com), where designer Patrick McNeil tracks current trends in colors and designs of popular websites. His groupings of similarly themed websites are especially helpful if you have no idea where to start. If it interests you, spend some time perusing the different sites and colors, and reading the analyses. The more knowledge you have, the better.

## In Black and White

Using a moderate amount of color as accent and/or to frame different pieces of content can make the impact you desire without oversaturating your design or cluttering your pages with colored text and colored or patterned backgrounds. Black text against a white background is always a safe bet. It's easy to read and easy on the eyes, promoting user readability and decreasing the risk of eyestrain. In fact, colored text on a colored or, heaven forbid, a patterned background can actually drive users away. People can look at bright yellow text on a purple background covered with polka dots for only so long before their eyes start to bulge and their heads start to throb.

I tend to use white or subtle colors and dark text in my designs, simply because it's easier for people to see and doesn't cause eyestrain. I recommend you do the same and just stick with a black (or at least dark) type on a white (or at least light) background.

I also recommend putting white space around images and between different sections of your page, to help guide the users' eye from one part of your page to the next. If your pages are crammed with stuff and the different sections seem to run together, they can be overwhelming to look at and it can be difficult for users to discern one piece of content from another. At a certain point, users reach a point of visual overload and just need to give their eyes a break . . . which means, they're out of there. For an example of this, please go back and visit one of my original Top Five Sites, Apple Computer (www.apple.com). Apple designers are masters at the use of space in design.

To reiterate, because these don'ts are so important to good design (and because these design faux pas are too frequently made), remember:

**Don't use clashing colors.** Certain colors should never be used together (like green and red, or blue and orange, or anything you might consider "clownish"—unless, of course, your intent is for your site to be loud and obnoxious because such a look serves your target audience and your brand well. For instance, if you're catering to video-game-playing fifteen-year-old boys, I'd say use as much bold color and high-end technology as you want. For the most part, though, weird color combinations should be avoided. Not only can clashing colors annoy and offend users, they can cause migraines, make the text hard to read, and distract from your content. You get only one chance to make a first impression; make sure your color scheme jibes with the impression you want to make on your primary users. As a rule of thumb, use the web-safe colors found in Dreamweaver, FrontPage, and other web development programs.

**Don't use patterned backgrounds.** Feathers, beads, multiple squares, or anything that makes the text hard to read should be avoided like the plague. These might look cool while you're considering different design elements for your site, but they create eyestrain and have "amateur" written all over them. Even if you want your site to project a down-home image and you're selling homemade products there, you don't want users to think of your site or your business as anything less than professional. In this case, simpler is definitely better.

**Don't use heavy, patterned, or otherwise noticeable borders.** Creating visual dissonance on the site breaks concentration. You want users to focus on the words, not the design.

**Don't use too much black.** White type on a black background might look cool when you first see it, but after reading a few lines, it quickly causes eyestrain, because black absorbs light. Not only is it difficult to read, it can distract from and seem to swallow the images and other content.

**Text should not blink, scroll, or move in any other way.** It's great if you know how to make it do this, but users are not impressed with a site that looks like a shoot-the-duck booth at a carnival. If you make text hard to read, it will not be read.

# Design Standards

Even in the ever-changing world of the Internet, there are certain standards that you're better off sticking with. Most users will tolerate only a certain amount of pushing the envelope before they get annoyed or confused and go elsewhere. People tend to prefer the familiar to the avant-garde. When given the choice between something they know works and something unknown, they're more than likely going to choose the same-old same-old, even if the new rendition looks better. I'm talking here about things that break tradition, like a flashing shopping cart or some navigation that disappears when you roll over it, or anything else that might seem cool, but is likely just to annoy your users, who are just going to your site to get something done.

So it is with link colors, buttons, and other Internet standards. Stray too far from the norm and not even your most tech-savvy users will follow you. Trying to get fancy with and deviating from certain conventions that people have come to know, if not love, will end up doing you more harm than good.

Web design standards that you would be wise to follow include:

1. **Underline links and only links.** Any word (or group of words) that is underlined must be a clickable link. Do not underline headings and do not use underlining to emphasize a word or phrase within text; instead, use bigger, bold, italic, or a different color type (except for the two standard link colors, on page 145). Internet users expect all links to be underlined and they expect all underlined text to be links. If a link is simply the standard color for links (blue) but not underlined, users might not realize it's a link. If they try to click on underlined text and it doesn't take them anywhere, they're going to think the link doesn't

work. Either way, you've given users cause for frustration and to question the integrity of your site.

2. **Link colors.** There are two standard colors for links: blue and purple. Is it possible to use other colors for links? Yes, and some sites do it well, but it is always a good idea to know the standards before you decide to push them. If you do vary from the blue/purple convention, use the same color for all the visited links and the same color for all the unvisited links on your site—and *always* underline each link. I'm not convinced that users are savvy enough to know that a blue word that isn't underlined is a link, and I know they won't recognize an orange word that is not also an underlined word as a link. Underlining is an absolute must and blue is the standard color option for links. You don't want to risk losing business because people are wondering, "Is that a link? Should I click on that word? What's going on here?"

3. **Button links.** A button that says "Buy Now" should allow users to click on it to take them to that link and does not need a text link next to it for the same purpose. Including both a button link and a text link for essentially the same command will make users think these are two different options—and will drive them crazy.

4. **Page size.** Again, you'd think this would be a no-brainer: Just make the page whatever size your program says it is or whatever size your designer made it, right? Wrong. Your site should be fixed-width 800 pixels x 600 pixels so that it fits in standard screens without creating the need for scrolling, or adjustable—meaning, it adjusts to fit the screen of the computer that's viewing it. You want to make sure your site falls within the 90th percentile of use, meaning you can see 90 percent of the site in the browser window on your computer when you have it in "full-screen" mode. Mostly what you don't want is for your user to have to scroll sideways in order to see the whole screen.

5. **Keep your file size under control.** Though many of us have long forgotten the days when we didn't have high-speed Internet access in our homes, offices, libraries, Internet cafés, and elsewhere, there are still people who access the web primarily through a dial-up connection. People in rural areas and in other countries,

for example, might not have the option of high-speed access, but they are still potential customers. If it consistently takes a long time to load your site because your image files are too big, you stand to lose those customers who don't have the latest in technology at their disposal. To minimize the size of your graphic files, save them as images "for the web." To re-size your images if they're too large, you can use any photo editing program—even one that came with your computer. Some examples of programs you can use to re-size photos include Fireworks, GoLive, Corel PaintShop Pro, and Microsoft Editor. "Save for Web" is very important, and will make a big difference in the overall usability of your site. Just open up the photo, click "Save for Web," re-save, then put it back up on your site the way you originally put it there.

6. **Use photos of real people.** Speaking of photos and images, one trend that's really caught on over the years is the use of real people's photographs throughout websites, and especially on homepages, which helps to cut through the technology and give customers a human connection. Your customers are real people, and the use of real faces on your website makes it instantly more accessible. If you're curious as to who is using this technique, I would encourage you to visit "Top Ten Online Retailers," which you can find on the blog of marketing firm FutureNow (www .grokdotcom.com/category/conversion-rates). Recent examples of this phenomenon have included retail giants Zales, QVC, and LifeLock, a company that sells identity theft protection. What better place to have real people?

The interaction of real people is also very important to the growth of a website, and will be covered in Chapter 11, as there are many great tools out there that will allow you to incorporate the personal element through your actual users.

7. **Scale the technology and design based on the user.** After all the talk about color and branding and what's appropriate for what target audience, there is one thing I can tell you for certain: The older your target demographic, the simpler you're going to need to make your site. Simply put, the baby boom generation didn't

grow up with computers, and they have almost no tolerance for super-fancy technology. Think of this as an inversely proportional curve—the older your ideal user is, the less technology you should use. People can debate me on this all they want, but after more than a decade in web design and development (and a 101-year-old grandmother-in-law who loves her email), I have yet to see a website that caters to the fifty and older set succeed through the use of complicated technology. Remember, the older your target audience, the more simple and clear your site needs to be.

## Let's Get It Started!

Okay, you understand all the design concepts outlined in this chapter, and you're ready to apply them to your site. Maybe your site also has one or more of the more long-term fatal flaws discussed in Chapter 7, and now it's time to correct them. Maybe you've decided to take what you've learned and completely start over. Armed with the guidelines from this chapter, you'll be able to either design (or redesign) your site yourself, have a friend do it, or hire a professional firm to do it.

Now is the time to open up your site and start making some changes, or to redesign entirely. Decide on the web development software (Adobe Dreamweaver is always on my list), or choose the do-it-yourself program you're going to use (like TypePad, Intuit's Homestead, GoDaddy's WebSite Tonight, or one of the many others out there). Take out the notes you've been compiling about your site as we've gone over concepts in previous chapters. Start working within your site to change navigational structure, edit content, and reduce clutter. If you're thinking of a whole redesign, start experimenting with new layouts and colors that more accurately convey your vision and appeal to your target audience. If your site is built out of image files, copy and paste the text into some regular pages.

If you don't have the time, inclination, or skill to design and build your site yourself, you have two other options: Find someone you know to do it inexpensively (or help you if you get stuck) or hire a pro. Whatever you decide, you should go into the redesign armed with everything you've developed so far—feedback from your current site, your Top Five Sites list and what you like about them, user scenarios that you've developed for your primary audience, your information architecture (if you've created a new one), and any writing you've done for the site. This is the moment! You are ready to put all your new elements together to make your brand-new site.

But first, a word.

If there is one thing I would like you to take away from this book, it's that your website is yours, and that you should never be "afraid" of it or feel like it's out of your hands. I hate to see small business people lose control of this valuable tool because "only the web person understands how to update it" or because they run out of money to pay a designer. Just because you don't have an in-depth knowledge of design and HTML, don't let that stop you from trying. You and your website can grow together. Start where you are, and you'll find that the whole thing is much easier than you thought. When well-constructed, your website should function as a living, breathing part of your organization that can change as often as you want it to.

With all of this said, if you're going to hire someone (or get someone else) to make your site for you, here is my one request: Please make sure that you understand how to make changes to the site once the designer gives it to you. It may come to you in the form of HTML pages. If that's the case, start familiarizing yourself with a program like Dreamweaver or another HTML editor. Your website is going to need continued care and attention, and unless you have the budget to keep paying someone to update it (and if you do, fantastic), you're going to need some skill, or you'll end up in the same place a few years from now. Take the power back now!

Here's how to go about finding someone to put it all together for you, should you choose to go in that direction.

### Hire a Friend or Student

There is nothing wrong with having a friend with some design experience who's trying to break into the business make your website for cheap or with finding a design student willing to do your site for his or her portfolio. You might even want to add a "web development intern" to your business, who can learn on the job and build a portfolio. The easiest way to find these eager people is by putting an ad on Craigslist (www.craigslist.com) or calling your local design school or university's web design department to see if they have any students who need work to build up their portfolios. Just make sure you are extremely clear about your vision of the brand and the site and about all the guidelines discussed up until now. You definitely don't want to turn the project over to a student only to discover he or she has redesigned you a whole new site in Flash. Remember, just because you're not designing the site yourself doesn't mean you should lose control of the project. Supervise this person closely, give feedback immediately, and make sure he or she will be available to make changes for you once you start getting feedback from others, or that you've learned enough about web development by then to make the updates yourself.

### Hire a Pro

If you decide that hiring a pro is the best approach for you, you have a variety of good options to choose from—depending on what your budget is, what you're trying to accomplish, and how much technology you need on your site. Here are a few basic guidelines for choosing a company to develop your website:

1. **What else have they done?** The company you hire to create your site should have enough experience designing and building websites that are similar to what you're looking for. Check out the websites they've done to make sure they not only look good but also function well. You'll notice that certain companies will have certain aesthetics that seem to run through everything they make, which is fine if you like what they do. However, if everything they create looks like a video game and you sell furniture, keep looking, no matter how versatile they claim to be.
2. **Are the costs reasonable?** Always ask for a cost estimate, and always get cost estimates from more than one designer. You don't want

to overextend your budget on the design and development and then not have any money to put into advertising and promotion. If you've never had someone build a website for you before and you don't know if the costs sound reasonable, the best idea is to get two or three estimates, so you can compare them.

3. **Are they willing to collaborate with you?** This is very important. You're taking the initiative to learn more about what works on websites. If they're not willing to listen to suggestions or answer your questions, or if they are overly pushy or insistent on a certain style that they recommend, move on.

Again, once they turn the site over to you, it's still going to need care and updates. Make sure you have the budget in place (or the skills) to guarantee that your site stays healthy and up-to-date.

## *Where to Find Designers*

You can look for designers in the same places that you look for writers (see Chapter 9). Choose the designer whose work you like, with whom you have a rapport, and who fits your budget. Chances are, you'll have your choice of good designers right in your own backyard. But don't let geography come between you and the designer of your choice. With modern technology, everything can be easily accomplished remotely—over the phone, fax, and Internet—and the need to meet face-to-face has almost become obsolete.

Here are places where you might find the designer to meet your needs:

**Word of mouth.** Start with your circle of friends and associates. If someone you know recommends a designer or firm that has worked well for them, talk to the designer about your project, get a quote, and see if it's within your budget.

**Craigslist.** Just like writers, there are designers in every city, some of whom have posted their resumes on Craigslist (in the "Resumes" section). Another option is to post an ad for a designer in the "Jobs" section (Craigslist charges for job listings in the biggest cities.) Advertise for a designer, and you'll get a slew of resumes and portfolios for your review. Choose a designer (or design firm) with a reasonable rate whose previous work you feel matches with your goals for your site. Ask the designer for an estimate for the whole site, and how much it will cost to provide periodic updates.

**Check out the online marketplaces.** These sites (previously mentioned in our discussion of where to find writers) are also great places to find designers and/or programmers to work on your project. Write up a summary of what you think you'll need, and make it available for bids. Or go to any of the sites and browse portfolios, and you'll quickly get a feel for whose design aesthetic and previous experience matches what you're going for. Check out www.allfreelancework .com, www.guru.com, www.elance.com, or www.odesk.com.

## Templates/Build-It-Yourself Sites

As I mentioned, I have nothing against these sites—in fact, I have seen many small businesses start out this way, then grow to the point where they're employing full-time graphic designers and programmers. One small business I know started out as a Mac.com site and is now part of a major media empire. So if this is what you want to do, this is 100 percent okay. Just be sure that your site is well organized and easy to navigate (Chapter 8) and the content is well written and relevant to your target audience (Chapter 9). And (from this chapter), when you get to the part where you need to actually choose the colors and the design, make sure you choose something that conveys your brand and speaks to your target audience/users. Some great all-in-one templates are Homestead (www .homestead.com), GoDaddy's WebSite Tonight (www.godaddy.com), and TypePad, which we'll be using to build Bob's new site.

The one quibble I have with build-it-yourself website templates is that they can tend to all look the same (because they're templates). So if you have the option, I would recommend mixing it up with some custom design, photography, your logo, or anything that will make your site stand out. Your intuitive architecture, good content, and user-focused design choices will make your site strong, but we also want to make sure it's memorable. For an example of this, let's go back to Bob, who has chosen to rebuild his site using a TypePad template. There, we'll see how easy it is to make a memorable site out of a preset design.

# REAL LIFE >>
## *Bob's Redesign*

THIS IS WHERE all of our previous work on Bob's site is going to pay off; that is, this is the part where we're going to utilize the new architecture and revamped content, and where we'll implement a brand-new design to show it all off. The last step in the process is to figure out what we're going to use to build the site. Bob doesn't want to repeat the experience he had last time (he doesn't know HTML, so he was afraid to make changes). Bob's had a bad taste in his mouth where his site is concerned since he never had the time to learn how to edit it, and he doesn't have the budget (yet) to pay someone to design his site and update it.

Based on all of these factors, I suggest that Bob rebuild his site using a program that will allow him to use some custom design (which I highly recommend) as well as being easy to use and organize. My feeling is that he should rebuild his site using TypePad, a blogging/website service I have helped clients use with great success. He goes into his redesign already successful because he's done all of the legwork of building a great site, from defining his target audience to building his keyword list to reorganizing his content into manageable sections to revamping all of his articles for the web. With TypePad he'll be able to easily put all of these elements together into an engaging site. And if he gets even more motivated and wants to push the envelope even further, TypePad offers a software program called Movable Type, which advanced users can download and use to make their own sites.

To start, we get him a TypePad account (www.typepad.com), and he goes to work.

Note: Bob's happy with the e-commerce (store) portion of his site (where people actually enter their credit card information and check out), which is handled by a third-party provider (Bob's using a Yahoo!

store). The "store" links on his site have always sent people over to his storefront there, and that's the way it's going to stay. The subject of merchant accounts and/or setting up a storefront goes beyond the scope of this book, but I've recommended several resources in Chapter 18 if you're stuck.

Bob's not just making a blog, so he joins TypePad as a "Professional" user, so he can have access to all of the tools (and can make as many sites as he wants).

Bob and I make a separate site (or blog, as TypePad will call it) called "Bob's Dogs." Then we designate the following categories (from the re-architecture we did in Chapter 8):

About Us
Bob's Blog
Friends
Knowledge
Shop

This structure allows Bob to put all of his content in manageable sections which will be easy for users to find. The "About Us" section is where he'll put a (very) brief history of his love of dogs, along with his store hours and location (with a map). "Bob's Blog," a new feature, is where he'll share recent discoveries in eco-friendly pet care (more on blogs in Chapter 11). "Friends" will feature a photo gallery of his favorite customers, and the results of his monthly photo contest on Flickr. "Knowledge" is where he'll put all of the articles he's been writing and accumulating to help with customers' questions; these will also help his site attract more people, as each of the articles will contain many of the keywords in the list he made in Chapter 3, which will make the site show up much higher in the search engines once he submits it (coming up in Chapter 16).

We hired a professional designer to create the banner that lives at the top, because it's very important to set the tone with good design no matter how simple or functional you're making your site.

The rest of the site, though, will be totally based on a template.

TypePad also makes it easy to manage the "constant" elements of the site—the pieces that are going to live permanently on either side of the site—what you put in the center will be what changes. They accomplish this through what they call "Typelists." For Bob's site, we create Typelists for the opt-in mailing list box. (We got this code from GetResponse.com back in Chapter 7 when we did the triage on Bob's site, and now we're just integrating it into the new design.)

New banner for Bob's site, by Miss Mary K

The main message (in the center) welcomes people to the site, keeps their focus, and engages them with a photo of a real little boy and his dog. He's also got a link right there on the homepage so that people can find and buy his most popular product, the Amazing HomeMade Biscuit. Using TypePad's simple technology, we include a module from Petfinder, which will allow him to refer those interested in adopting a pet over to their site. Overall, this is a great base for Bob to build on to his heart's desire; he can add as many articles as he likes to the "Articles" section, post frequent updates to Bob's Blog, and customers now have an easy way to find the online store and the directions to his brick-and-mortar location.

Put all the pieces together, and you've got a site that reflects Bob's "clean and simple" vibe, is easy to navigate, does a much better job engaging his customers, and will be easy for him to update.

Bob's site (shown before and after on page 155) is now better organized, much more scalable, and nicer to look at. He's going to continue to add as he learns more about TypePad, but already he's happy with the way the site looks, and is hopeful about all the cool stuff he can add in the future to make his users' experience the best it can be. Most important, Bob is excited about his website for the first time!

## Bob's Dogs site before:

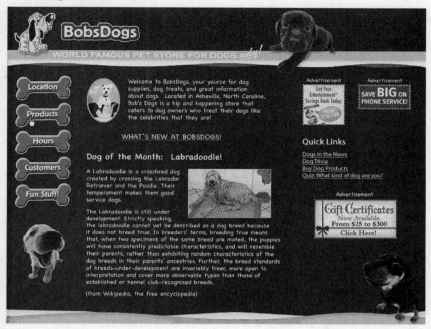

By Get Creative, Inc.

## Bob's Dogs site after:

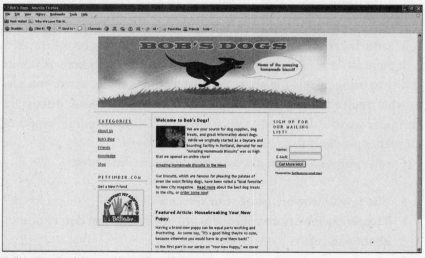

Built on Typepad, banner design by Miss Mary K

# 11 | Get Personal

Content from users can help create a community of loyal customers that places you high on their list of favorite sites.

**You're doing great!** Once you've tackled architecture, design, and writing, this part will be no problem. After all, you want as many people to see your now-awesome site as possible, right? Getting your community actively involved in the success of your site is another integral step in your plan for total website domination. This involves making your site interactive—meaning, users can contribute to it in one of a few ways. This will insure that once they find you, they will keep coming back forever.

If there is one thing for which the Internet is universally known, it is its ability to bring people together. No matter who you are, where you are, or what you're interested in, you can find a message board, discussion group, or website dedicated to your interests. This community aspect of the web is probably its greatest asset.

For the purposes of this discussion, community includes:

▶ The people who are using your site already
▶ The people for whom your site is intended (who just don't know about you yet)

In Internet Land, "integrating community into your site" means putting in one or more interactive components that get your users involved with your site or that create a community that interacts with one another on the site. From the users' standpoint, the most appealing aspects of being part of an online community are:

▶ Being in the company of like minds—people with similar interests and viewpoints
▶ Feeling like they are part of something bigger than themselves
▶ Getting the inside scoop on the latest and greatest in their field of interest

For a business site, the advantages of creating an online community—in providing a meeting place where like-minded people can network, chat, and exchange information—is that it builds brand recognition and customer loyalty.

A loyal customer who gives you years of repeat business is worth her or his weight in gold. In fact, one loyal customer who orders regularly is worth more than twelve customers who each make a one-time purchase, because for each of those twelve, you'll need to deduct the cost of acquisition—the dollars you spent to get the users to your site and convert them to customers. The repeat customer always means more money in your pocket, and a community of repeat visitors might just make you rich. Look at it this way: As I've mentioned earlier, a potential customer needs to be exposed to your brand and your products an average of *ten times* before he or she becomes your customer.

What if the community content on your site was so engaging that it brought users back twice a day *on their own*, until they essentially converted themselves? This would really free you up to do other things—like count your money.

When you invite users to become part of your community, you are, in essence, asking them to become part of your team. The more involved users are with your site, the more they'll use it and recommend it to others. Every business, whether you sell bird food, baby clothes, auto parts, or school supplies, has a core group of customers with similar interests. Your task in building an online community is to get those customers to interact with one another on your site.

In the early days of the Internet, creating an online community simply meant including a message board on your site on which people could post messages and conduct online discussions with other users. Now the term has expanded to include things like blogs (and the people who read and comment on them), user-generated content, and social networking. You'll also need to moderate your community content to make sure nothing untoward is going on. But in just letting people talk to one another via your site, you're building your own equity.

## Engaging Users with Community Features

Users love to feel like they're contributing to the overall experience of the site, whether it's by telling their story about how they like your product, sharing their personal experiences or knowledge, or just commenting on something they don't like. By involving your users on some level, you are ensuring several things:

**Free content.** When users are passionate about a community, they take pleasure in sharing information, knowledge, and stories to keep it alive and growing. This also ties in with the element of personalization we started talking about in the last chapter with the mention of including photographs of real people. Users love to be actively involved; they want you to want their stories, and they're thrilled when you include them in your site. Even if you have to give something away in order to get some good user-contributed content, it's well worth it in the long run for the positive associations, repeat traffic, and good recommendations you're going to get in return. This could come in the form of photos, articles written by "volunteers" who read your blog or love your site and just want to be a part of it, or the incorporation of a message board that takes on a life of its own, as it were.

**Free promotion.** When a users post their stories, knowledge, or just about anything else that is relevant on your website, they send everyone they know there to check it out. Let's say that two people out of that group of everyone-they-know love your site and become your customers. Great! That's two new customers for the price of free content. You win twice!

**Free repeat traffic.** Users who are engaged visit sites multiple times per day to communicate with one another. Once a user adds a photo, an opinion, or any other piece of personalized content, you can be sure that user is going to come back frequently to see what others think (and send everyone he or she knows to the site to see the contribution). Community involvement in a website is akin to planting seeds in a garden. As long as you water regularly, time will work its magic and you'll end up with beautiful flowers.

Following are some examples of ways in which different companies are using community to build and promote their sites. Make mental notes of anything that might work for your business.

## Jones Soda: Photos
*www.jonessoda.com/gallery*

Jones Soda makes soda, so you might not expect them to get the publicity and web traffic they have from what is essentially a photo contest. In 1995, in a promotional campaign designed to create an emotional connection between their products and consumers, Jones Soda started taking photo submissions and putting real people's pictures on their soda bottles. Several years ago they added an online component—the ability for users to post their photos and have people vote on them on the website—and they have received *millions* of submissions ever since. To this day, they have an ongoing contest, in which you can put a photo of yourself (or your child, dog, grandma, friend, coworker, neighbor, whomever) on their website and, if it gets enough votes, have your winning photo featured on the label of a limited-run bottle of Jones Soda.

Jones Soda archives the photos online for only six months, and at any given moment, there are well over half a million photos on this site. I don't need to tell you, that has translated into at least half a million visitors in the past six months, plus all the friends and family the photo contestants then send to the site to vote for their photos. Jones Soda could have bought that kind of traffic, but I'm guessing it would have cost a lot more than what they paid for the photo contest.

## About.com: Content
*www.about.com*

If you want an overview about just about anything, About.com is the place to go. About.com calls itself the Human Internet, and it uses experts ("guides," as they call them) to build each section. What's great about this model is that it's infinitely scalable—guides only get paid for their efforts based on page views, so About.com lets the experts build the individual sections and brands them all under the About.com umbrella. If you have an interest and expertise in a certain subject, definitely try to become an About.com guide. Whatever time you invest in building their site for them will pay off tenfold, once your traffic increases and you link to your own site from your expert area.

About.com is actually utilizing two community strategies in their site:

1. They let experts build and edit the content.
2. They encourage discussion among enthusiasts in their "Forum" section.

Combined, these two strategies produce hundreds of thousands of repeat visitors to About.com each year (and, most likely, millions of dollars in ad revenue).

## DiscoverNursing.com: Personal Profiles
*www.discovernursing.com*

When DiscoverNursing.com launched in 2002, it featured profiles and photos of fifty nurses. This section ended up being so popular that it was opened up for any and all nurses to add their own stories and photos. Now the site has more than three hundred profiles, and this section is by far the most popular on the site. Average visit length for the site is consistently over ten minutes, as users stay to read each and every unique journey toward becoming a nurse.

# What Kind of Community Is Right for You?

Okay, so you're convinced that harnessing the power of your community through some type of interactive feature is a good idea. But what type of interactive community feature is right for your users (and potential users)? That, my friend, is your community X factor. To be honest, there is a little bit of mystery involved in getting your community feature to catch on so that people are using it on a regular basis, telling their friends about it, and so on.

If you're not sure yet what your community X factor might be, don't worry about it; something will come to you over the course of this chapter. First, make sure your site is ready to host and develop its own online community by:

▸ Building a high-quality site that is content-rich and easy to navigate
▸ Driving traffic to your site and getting people used to visiting on a regular basis
▸ Keeping the content fresh, up-to-date, and engaging

Once you've got these elements down, then you can start working on the community aspect. In other words, don't skip all the other steps in the book, put a message board on your site, and call it a day. This will just make things worse, as people will use the message board to discuss how much your site sucks.

Of the many different types of community-building features you can incorporate in your site, probably the easiest to set up and maintain are message boards and blogs. Both of these basically involve facilitating interactive discussions on your site. Message boards achieve this by allowing visitors to freely post in response to topics (which may or may not have to do with your site). Blogs do this by engaging users with content you create and then allowing them to post comments.

# Blogs

Using a blog is an inexpensive way to draw people into your site, share your expertise on your subject, and let users share their opinions and comments. Many people have even built entire businesses around their blogs.

Blog software makes it easy for you to update your blog quickly and for people to comment on it right away, thereby engaging you in an ongoing conversation about your chosen topic (that's going to be filled with your keywords).

This essentially means you are providing expert advice and having a dialog with your users while you engage in a topic of mutual interest, and while you are promoting your products and raising your search engine rankings. For you, that is a win-win-win.

Your business might benefit from using a blog if any of the following apply:

▸ You have a lot of new information about your topic or business.
▸ You are already an authority in your field.
▸ You closely follow your industry.
▸ You are involved in an evolving or rapidly changing industry that a lot of people want to know about, like self-help, pop culture, or anything pertaining to being eco-friendly. If you're curious about what subjects are the most searched for on any given day, visit the Google Trends Lab (www.google.com/trends), where you'll find a list of the most popular searches of the moment.

If you enjoy writing frequent articles (or posts) about your field of expertise and you're active in the management of your site, a blog could be a great option for you. Your users will soon start consulting you as an authority on the subject. They will also be more likely to buy your products and to continue buying as they become familiar with you as an expert. By allowing users to post comments, you can gain insight, more content, and a connection that will keep them coming back for more. Eventually, you might want to have some of the more frequent posters come on as guest bloggers or editors. This will expand your user base even more (and add to the content of your site). Again, everybody wins.

You should not incorporate blogging into your website if you (or a member of your staff) are unable to make frequent (read, daily or at least weekly) posts. The whole concept of blogging started as an easy way to keep an online journal, and that is still its main purpose. If you're going to update once a month, at least disable the date function so your users can't tell how infrequently you post.

Blogging technology, used correctly and cleverly, can be used as an inexpensive content management system that will allow you to easily update your site. Once your site is being visited regularly by the search engines, new posts will count as new content and will be indexed immediately. It is also rumored within industry circles that Google might be giving a slightly higher preference to content on Blogger.com sites since it owns Blogger, but I've also seen good results with LiveJournal and TypePad posts getting into the search engines right after they're published (on already established sites).

## Starting a Blog

The most popular services that offer do-it-yourself blogging services are Blogger, LiveJournal, and TypePad. Each has its own advantages and disadvantages, based on what features you're looking to use and/or what you're willing to pay. I would recommend trying each of them out (all are either free or offer a free trial) and seeing which one you like the most.

Blogger (www.blogger.com). Blogger was a small company that exploded with the popularization of the blog, and it is now owned by Google. Since it's free, Blogger is probably the easiest way to incorporate blogging into your site today. However, as with any free technology, Blogger has a limited number of templates and cannot be as easily changed to match your site. Still, if it's just an online journal you're after, Blogger is the way to go.

LiveJournal (www.livejournal.com). With more than 16 million journals and communities created since 1999, LiveJournal has a huge number of users and a growing list of features for new bloggers. LiveJournal offers a free account that can be upgraded if you want to use more of the features.

**TypePad (www.typepad.com).** A newer service than Blogger, TypePad charges a subscription fee that varies with the number of blogs you have. With more choices for design, a useful statistics function, and a very helpful customer service desk, TypePad has started to gain ground over the free blogging sites.

Here's how to get a crash course in blogging and incorporate it into your business right now:

1. Go to Blogger.com and open an account (free).
2. Give your blog a name that contains your business name. For instance, Bob's Dogs might choose the blog name http:// bobsdogblog.blogspot.com.
3. Look through the design templates and select one that at least suggests the design of your site. You don't want your users thinking they've completely left your universe when they go from the site to the blog or vice versa.
4. Familiarize yourself with the software by writing several informative posts. These can be personal anecdotes, recipes, how-to tips, or anything relevant to your users and well written. Remember, you are trying to engage readers so that they will become your customers, so keep it professional and don't talk about what you had for lunch.
5. When you are satisfied with the content and appearance of your blog, create a navigational link to your main site, preferably on the homepage.

Having a blog on your site will indicate to new users that you have expertise in your field and have something interesting to say. It will also give existing customers a reason to come back and share their opinions. If, after trying out Blogger, you find that it's not keeping up with your needs, try the thirty-day free trial of TypePad. Though you do have to pay for this service, TypePad offers so many more features, it's definitely worth it. With TypePad's customizable features, you can come much closer to approximating the look of your site. Plus, TypePad will help you seamlessly integrate into your blog everything from Google AdWords to a tip jar, to book recommendations and everything in between.

## Blogs in Action

Check out these informative and effective blogs:

**CardPlayer.com (www.cardplayer.com).** Poker champion Daniel Negreanu boasts an impressive number of visitors to his blog, which also happens to be linked to (and sponsored by) CardPlayer .com. People come to the site for the blog, because they want to know how this master plays poker. Presumably they end up buying the products while they're there.

**Celebrity Baby Blog (www.celebritybabies.com).** The Celebrity Baby Blog (CBB) is another impressive blog that features constantly updated photos of pregnant celebrities and celebrities with their kids. With good writing, consistent updates, and a strong moderator, CBB is one of the most successful upstart media outlets out there, often breaking celebrity news before *People* magazine and E! Online. This advantage is surely the result of good editors combined with loyal readers. (When a piece of news breaks, editors receive hundreds of emails from readers.) The Celebrity Baby Blog has several contributors (most of whom graduated from being regular readers) and many regular advertisers, and gets millions of unique visitors and page views each month. Celebrity Baby Blog is also one of the million dollar website winners—originally started as a simple TypePad blog for creator Danielle Friedland in 2004 to share her extensive knowledge of celebrity pregnancies and babies, CBB grew so much that in 2008 it was sold to Time, Inc. (owner of *People* magazine) for a deal that was reported to be in the "low millions." Friedland and staff stayed on as editors, while Time took over and revamped the site.

**Dooce (www.dooce.com).** Writer/designer Heather Armstrong is the creator of the mega-popular blog Dooce.com, which she started in 2001. This blog is mostly dedicated to Armstrong's personal life, and took off when she was fired from her job for blogging about her co-workers, putting the term "dooced" firmly in the cultural vernacular. Her frank discussions of everything from her daughter to the post-partum depression that landed her in a psychiatric hospital are good examples of the kind of personal stories and content that keep readers coming back for more. Case in point: Dooce.com is one of the most popular blogs in the world. According to Google, 66,000 other sites point to Dooce, and Federated Media (which handles advertising for the site) estimates traffic to the site at more than 4 million page views per month (a tough statistic to pin down, but impressive nonetheless). An example of the power of Dooce? Armstrong recently did a Nintendo Wii promotional giveaway which users could enter by leaving a comment. By the time the entry period was over, she'd gotten more than 42,000 entries. Yes, it took time to build that readership, but the power's in the numbers. Right now, Dooce has it.

# Discussion Boards/Forums

Messages boards (or forums), are a great way to get your users engaged and create repeat visitors.

You might want to think about including a forum section in your site if:

▶ Your product or business is related to a subject that is ongoing and that people like to discuss with frequency, such as travel, pregnancy, dieting, or any kind of self-help product.
▶ You need to develop a lot of content. Often, the users who come back to message boards and post frequently are experts.
▶ You can learn a great deal from your message board users and possibly recruit (or hire) some of them to write for your site. At the very least, following the discussion threads can be a great education for you.

## Adding a Forum/Message Board to Your Site

Register with a service like Boardhost (www.boardhost.com) or Website Toolbox (www.websitetoolbox.com/message_board). Some message boards can be added to your site for free; these are free by being "ad-supported," so make sure you're okay with having advertising on your board over which you have no control (though they will try to make the ads content-related just to make them as successful as possible). A better option is to pay the small fee to integrate the board with your site and make yourself the moderator. Since you're paying for it and it's on your site, you'll have the right to edit and remove content, as well as run your own ads.

Set up initial topics, such as "Welcome," "Introduce Yourself," and any specific issues that your site might deal with.

If you're not sure if a message board is right for your site, try starting with one that's free, then, if it really catches on, upgrading to a "paid" board over which you'll have more control.

## Forums in Action

Here are some more examples of well-done forums:

**The Caregiver Initiative (www.strengthforcaring.com).** Strength for Caring, part of the Caregiver Initiative created by Johnson & Johnson, is an online resource and community for family caregivers. This is an excellent example of how *and* why to use a message board. Caregivers (those caring for the ill or elderly) can benefit tremendously from one another's knowledge, and can use the message board as a place to connect with others dealing with similar issues. Strength for Caring gives participating members moral support, exchange of helpful information, and a sense of being part of something larger than oneself.

**Oprah.com (www.oprah.com).** Oprah has built a hugely successful media empire, is a television and movie producer, has a radio show, and is changing the world with webcasts. Is there anything she can't do? Another thing she's doing really successfully is engaging her community; at any given time there are tens (maybe hundreds) of thousands of people in the forums on her site, discussing everything from today's show topic to religion to the latest Oprah's Book Club pick. Oprah knows that her audience has something to say, and she's given them the place to do it, further adding to her global media domination. If you're going to emulate someone, please, let it be Oprah.

**BabyCenter.com: Community Discussions** (www.babycenter.com/community). One thing web developers have learned about the Internet over the years is that if you give people a forum, they'll talk to one another. This is perhaps best demonstrated when the subject is babies, children, and pregnancy (subjects that have a lot of "firsts" and therefore new subject matter). BabyCenter.com is a destination site for women who are trying to get pregnant, expectant mothers, new moms, moms with two or more children, and the like. It's a great place to share the experience of pregnancy and motherhood with other people living the same experience. (And it's great that their store is always prominently displayed in the navigation, in case you want to buy something.) BabyCenter.com has great traffic and a large number of repeat users.

**Personal Development for Smart People/StevePavlina.com** (www.stevepavlina.com). Self-help author and expert Steve Pavlina has made great use of his community to spur his blog and website on to huge success. In 2004 Pavlina started the site, which includes a blog, forum, newsletter, and hundreds of self-help articles. Within six months, he was averaging $4.12 per day in revenue from the Google Ads he had up there. Cut to three years later—Pavlina's site has an extremely effective forum called Personal Development for Smart People, which has more than 16,000 members discussing everything from the law of attraction to organic diets to world affairs. He's also kept up with adding tons of new content to the site and using many of the search engine strategies we discuss here. The end result? As of fall 2008, Steve

Pavlina's site is getting 2.5 million visitors per month and making a five-figure income (monthly). He's got some great articles on his site about how he did it—definitely visit the forum for fascinating discussions of all topics.

# Photos/Photo Contests

Having users contribute photos (as in the Jones Soda example) is a fun and engaging way to get your community involved while you expand your content. It's even better if you combine each photo with a personal story, but a photo gallery works well too (preferably with captions so the user doesn't feel adrift in the world of the photos). All you really need to do this is a Flickr Pro (www.flickr.com) account (not the free one, which only holds two hundred images). Form a group that others can join so that they, too, can upload photos and share in the fun.

Consider integrating a photo contest or other photo upload component if:

▶ **You have a product or service that lends itself well to photography.** Fashion and beauty products are naturals for photography. But even products that might not seem to lend themselves to photography can be good candidates, with the right campaign—such as with Jones Soda. Users love the immediacy of being able to see their photos on your site.

▶ **You want to create a personal connection between what you're selling and your consumers.** There is perhaps no better way to get people involved than to put their picture and story on your website. Just make sure it's relevant to your business, or users will know you're just doing it for the free publicity. Unilever made great use of real photographs in the "Dove Campaign for Real Beauty," during which they collected and displayed thousands of photos of real women (proving their point that beauty comes in many different forms).

▶ **You simply want to increase user interaction to that next level.** Everyone has had the experience of spending an entire afternoon on Facebook or a friend's website, looking at photos. It would be great to re-create that experience on your own site. Oprah is also employing this strategy; on Oprah.com, users are encouraged to upload inspirational photos, which can be put into slide shows and viewed by anyone who uses the network. Not only is this is a great way for photographers to get their work seen, but it forms a (seemingly infinite) pool of images to choose from. Yet another way that Oprah is doing it right!

## User-Generated Content

Inviting users to contribute content to your website can be a great way to get them to connect with your business and your site, which will keep them coming back for more. As with any community, you'll have users who are actually experts in your field, and as your site catches on, you'll start to hear from them (especially if you have a message board or blog with comments). There are many ways to get your users to contribute— writing contests, the offer of paid positions, or simply putting out a call for contributors on the site. Regular users of a site are often happy to contribute—for them, it means getting published, getting to control the quality of a site they like, and making a name for themselves in their field. Unlike the photo upload, however, I recommend not allowing people to post articles or content directly to your site. You need to be able to read and, if necessary, edit any content before you put it on your site, to make sure it fits your primary users and the tone of the site—and if it doesn't, to have the option not to include it at all. If you use other people's work on your site, you give them credit (a byline) and have them sign a release if necessary.

If you're still not sure what kind of community interaction functionality might work for your site, go back to your Top Five list or look at the sites of some of your competitors. What are they doing that's working? Once you figure out this element, you will harness the power of your community and your site will start to grow and flourish beyond your wildest dreams.

# Use Video to Attract Users

If you have a commercial, a piece of instructional video, or even a short piece of Flash animation that is somehow related to your business, getting it out there is a great way to attract new users to your site. Make sure that the video clip contains a reference to your URL (ideally clickable, so people who love the video can go right to the site), and upload it to the following:

**Google Video:** http://video.google.com
**YouTube:** http://youtube.com
**MySpaceTV:** http://vids.myspace.com

These days, video is so easy to shoot and edit and has the potential to reach so many people, I encourage everyone with a website to think of something they can put out there, just to increase exposure. You never know—you could capture a huge number of audience members with your "How to Make a Thanksgiving Turkey" video clip. If you run a cooking website, this could mean thousands of new users for you. This is a real example, by the way.

# Social Networking for Business Success

If you're one of the few people who haven't yet established a presence on MySpace, Facebook, LinkedIn, or one of the other numerous social networking sites, now's the time. Depending on your product/service and your target demographic, you might want to have one or more of these accounts. For now, spend some time visiting each one, looking around, and asking yourself: "How can I share my product or service with this audience?" Social networking is also a great place to put your energy if you don't have a huge advertising budget yet. It's absolutely free to build a network of hundreds of thousands of "friends" on MySpace who might be interested in your product. If you've got the time, they've got the people.

**MySpace (www.myspace.com).** If the target audience for your product includes people in the eighteen- to twenty-five-year-old demographic, you'll want to have a MySpace page that looks roughly like your site or product, talks a little about you, and links people back to your site. The music industry was the first to catch on to the amazing opportunity MySpace offers in one-to-one marketing. MySpace is a great resource for expanding the audience for your product or service one person at a time, but you really have to put in the energy. Don't expect to set up a generic MySpace page and attract a million "friends." Take the time to explore what your competition is doing on MySpace. Set goals for friends, reach out, post blogs, and make your page as interesting as possible.

**LinkedIn (www.linkedin.com).** LinkedIn's philosophy is that "your professional relationships are the key to your professional success." From their site: "LinkedIn is an online network of more than 15 million experienced professionals from around the world, representing 150 industries." What could be easier than writing a short profile of yourself—a profile that points those 15 million experienced professionals back to your killer website? Remember, your business (via your website) should be available to be seen as many places as possible. You never know who could be looking.

**Facebook (www.facebook.com).** Facebook is also a site based on networking, though it's more based on people you already know (either personally, through coworkers, or through mutual friends). If you've got something you're selling, whether a product, a service, or a brand-new company, you'll want everyone you've ever known to hear about it, so definitely sign up for Facebook and get back in contact with some old coworkers and high school friends. You never know who might be the key to your business taking off like a rocket.

**Twitter (www.twitter.com).** Twitter is a fun site that's rapidly gaining in popularity. A Twitter account is the equivalent of a little "news feed" all about you, which can be updated from a mobile source as well as the regular Internet. If you're familiar with the Facebook feed, then Twitter should be no problem to grasp. Basically you're feeding your audience little updates about you all day long, which keeps you in the forefront of their minds. If this sounds like fun to you, then sign up right away. Twitter is a great tool to keep users in touch with what you're doing, which is especially helpful if what you're doing has something to do with your business.

It seems that new social networking sites are cropping up every day, and while they're all fun and useful in their own right, using too many of them at once can get a little bit overwhelming. If you're in doubt, ask a member of your target demographic. If you cater to teenage girls and you don't know about Twitter, you are losing out on a whole world of marketing potential.

# REAL LIFE >>
## *Bob Builds His Community*

BOB AND I discuss different community-building options. He's dedicated to doing at least three blog postings per week, which will help build repeat traffic to his site as people come back to see what he has to say about eco-friendly pet care. I've also requested that he include audience-engaging questions at the end of every blog post, to encourage readers to get involved and comment. After a time, he should be able to get some guest bloggers to start posting content, as there are quite a few eager dog enthusiasts out there. (He knows this because they email him all the time.)

For the "real person" element, Bob has a great photo collection of his canine customers and their owners. I suggest that he start a photo contest on Flickr of people and their dogs, and that every month, the winning entry be featured on the homepage (the winner could also receive a free package of biscuits for the honor). This will accomplish the goal of making the first-time user want to engage immediately with this business (by entering a picture in the photo contest, then returning to see if it won). While the user is at it, hopefully she or he will become interested by one of the articles or Bob's blog, and will become a regular user of the site.

Setting up a Flickr account is easy to do (www.flickr.com), and to start this contest, Bob will just need to establish a "Group" within his Flickr account. Because he's hopefully going to get more than two hundred entries, he'll need to sign up for the Flickr Pro account (which charges a small monthly fee).

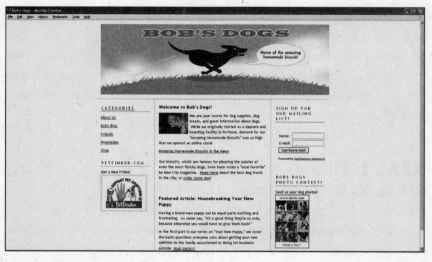

Built on Typepad, banner design by Miss Mary K

Bob should also allow his users to choose the winner of the monthly photo contest, which they can do by commenting on the Flickr site. As these community features start to take root on his site, we'll see what else we can do for Bob in social networking land.

With a little prodding, Bob also signs up for a Facebook account, since he's already committed to the blogging and maintaining his site and doesn't want to get in over his head with MySpace and Twitter as well. I would suggest the same for you—pick one social network-ing site just to get your feet wet. If you love it, then do more. Bob is delighted to discover that before long he has one hundred friends on Facebook and has reconnected with many people he's lost touch with. He'll include a link to his site and a little summary of what he's doing lately in his profile, and will join "dog lover" groups on Facebook, which will make it easier to connect with other people who might want to buy his products (and who share his love of dogs and the environment). Facebook should be a good fit for him, since it's got a slightly older and more professional demographic than MySpace. I remind him that he'll want to update the Facebook feed with dog-related or eco-friendly pet-related things pretty frequently, and he adds this to his calendar.

# 12 | Add Revenue with Ads

Judicious use of advertising on your site can improve your customers' experience while boosting your income.

**N**ow that you've gotten your website strategy straight, made some changes to make it more user-friendly, added some great content, honed your design, and started building a community, you might want to think about putting in some advertisements to add additional revenue streams. Through several different forms of advertising (affiliate marketing and text ads being the most popular), you are essentially getting paid to drive traffic to other people's sites. If you have a lot of users that shop online, for instance, you could make a decent secondary income by referring them to new shopping sites (assuming, of course, that these sites aren't competing with your products).

Affiliate marketing is basically advertisement by endorsement/referral. In exchange for you sending people to their sites, many companies will pay you a fee for these leads or a commission if the person you refer buys something. The common thinking behind this strategy is "If a customer leaves your site to go to another site, you should get paid for it."

The objectives of affiliate marketing are:

**1.** Create additional revenue streams from your site.

**2.** Increase the value that users place on your site by providing desirable referrals.

**3.** Add credibility to your site by associating yourself with major brands.

There are several different ways to use affiliate marketing in your site:

**Banner ads.** These are provided by the advertiser and appear directly on your site; all you do is cut and paste the code, and the ad starts appearing right away.

**Text linking.** A "text link" is created when you take the affiliate URL provided by the advertiser and incorporate (embed) it into the content on your site as an "active" link that goes over to the affiliate. If they make a sale based on this referral, you get a commission or referral fee. Embedded links look like this sentence, which might appear on the website of, say, a nutritionist or person who sold diet products: "The South Beach Diet was originally designed for heart patients, and then was so effective at lowering people's cholesterol and keeping weight off that it became an internationally bestselling book, a line of food, and a hugely popular website." In this example, a "South Beach Diet" link goes directly to a signup page on the South Beach Diet website. Your users sign up; you, as the referring site, make money.

**Google AdSense.** With this type of advertising, which works a little like a dating service for businesses and advertisers, you are matched up (by Google or a similar service) with advertisers whose products or services would appeal to your target audience. Those advertisers then display their text links on your site and pay you a per-click-through (referral) fee when your customers visit their sites. The text ad is certainly the most harmless of your advertising options and is an effective way to make a little extra money on your site without much work. Google AdSense offers one of the simplest signup processes, and has several options for getting links up on your site right away. You'll just need to know how to copy and paste some simple code into the site, and Google will provide the ads. After that, it's just a matter of logging in to see how much you've earned. Visit www.google.com/adsense for more information.

The affiliate marketing and advertising "games" have really taken off in the last few years, with many people claiming overnight riches simply through advertising and affiliate revenue. Though I wouldn't necessarily recommend going to that extreme, adding some affiliate marketing and/or advertising links to your site is a great way to provide added value to your customers, build your own brand equity, and make your site generate more income.

"Sounds like a good deal! Where do I sign up?"

We'll get to that in a moment, but first let's look at a few potential pitfalls of having other people's advertisements on your website.

Although affiliate marketing and/or text advertising on your site can be very lucrative, having too many links can do you more harm than they're worth. As a word of caution, when developing an advertising plan for your site, make sure that:

- ▶ Your site doesn't become merely a shopping mall of referrals to other sites. I've seen people do a ton of good work on their sites in terms of strong information architecture, keyword-loaded writing, and excellent design choices, and then ruin the whole thing by filling up the new site with twelve garish, distracting ads. Know when to say when.
- ▶ The target market for the products or companies to which you are referring your users is the same as the target market you've defined for your brand and site. You've worked hard to develop your brand and design your site for that market. Don't dilute or distort your message by putting anything on the site that isn't appropriate to your primary user. Just keep this in mind when you're picking advertisers to go on your site. Google AdSense actually has a content tool that will automatically match up the content on your site with the most appropriate ads.

▶ The text link advertisements are embedded into the content so as not to be distracting, and the blocks of text ads (or banner ads) don't appear right in the middle of an article or page. No one looks at a page full of banner ads, promotional copy for embedded links, and text ads. In most cases, it is preferable to include a piece of linked text referring the user to another site or provide text ads on the sides of the page, rather than putting up another company's banner ads. Here's why: After a while, your users aren't even going to be "seeing" the banners anyway. The usability experts at the Nielsen Norman Group have even introduced a term regarding this issue: "banner blindness." Simply put, your brain can only process so many banner ads before it just stops seeing them. So the more ads you put on your site, the less your users' brains are going to be engaged. Nothing scares users away faster than a page full of advertisements. At least give them some real content along with the ads.

## Affiliate Marketing How-tos

For this section, let's assume you've already got a website and you just want to add revenue streams in the form of referrals of some kind. For instance, you run a baby clothes website and provide links to BabyCenter, Gerber, and others. You get paid for the referrals and your customers are happy because they like your site and you recommend some great additional products. Everyone wins!

If you want to make a site specifically dedicated to affiliate marketing—meaning, you don't sell anything on your site and your only income is derived from referrals—you would do well to get one of the great books on this topic listed in Chapter 18. For that type of affiliate marketing, you'll need to pick a theme, calculate profit potential, sign up for affiliate programs, and build your whole website around that strategy.

What I'm talking about now is adding affiliate revenue to your existing site, from which you derive income by providing content, products, and/or services. Here is how to add some affiliate revenue to that type of site right now:

1. **Join a network.** First, you'll need to join an affiliate network. The largest one of these is Commission Junction (www.cj.com). If you were only going to join one network, I would recommend this one. Commission Junction has tens of thousands of advertisers, is well known, and pays regularly. Opening your Clickbank account is free and takes a few minutes. For a more complete list of affiliate networks, see Chapter 18. For now, join Commission Junction, just to see if this interests you and you like it. They have more than enough programs to get you started.

2. **Research potential affiliates.** Once you're a member of Commission Junction (or another network), spend some time searching for companies or products that are appropriate for your target audience and complement your brand, but that do not compete directly with your business. Remember: If someone is leaving your site, you want them to be generating money for you and you want them to come back.

3. **Join affiliate programs.** Even though you're a member of the Commission Junction network, you still need to join each advertiser's program separately, like the Gap, Crate & Barrel, and so forth. They'll send you an email once you're approved. Before applying to any of these programs, make sure your site is ready and in working order, because some of them actually come to your site to check it out before approving you. As long as you don't have any content they find objectionable, you're usually in.

4. **Choose ads and links.** Commission Junction has a good, one-stop-shopping interface, where you can get banner ads of all shapes and sizes (free) for inclusion on your site. You can do this by doing a manual "Save As" for the banner you like and then placing it in your site (where you'll then need to associate the appropriate referral link), or you can just copy the code for the banner ad and the referral text and stick it right into the code for your pages. If you're interested in this and want a more in-depth explanation, visit the extensive tutorial section on Commission Junction's site.

# Choosing Banner Ads

Since I know some people like banner ads and are going to keep using them despite my warning, the least I can do is offer some advice on choosing them correctly. Banner ads can be a great advertising stream for your site. Just be sure to choose them carefully so that they don't backfire by diluting your message and creating visual clutter on your site. When searching for and considering any and all banner ads for your site, remember to consider the following:

▶ **Does this product/service appeal to my target audience?** I can't emphasize this enough: Don't jeopardize your own site by putting up ads that are inappropriate to your user base. As discussed in Chapters 1 and 2, your users will think you don't know them, don't care about them, or have sold them out if they see ads that are totally inappropriate for them.

▶ **Is the banner ad from a well-known company?** Though some experts might debate me on this, I recommend not running ads for small and relatively unknown businesses on your site if you're a small business yourself. Associating yourself with large, reputable companies is the best way to create additional income while building your own brand equity. Choose ads for complementary brands that add to your credibility and exposure. Remember, that's your customer you're sending to the other site. If they have a bad experience, they're going to blame you. Conversely, if they have a great experience or find a great new site, they will remember you. Plus, you will get the money for the referral.

▶ **Does this banner ad fit the overall theme of my content?** Banner ads should follow the theme you've created for the site, both in design, color, style, and the language used in the ad. Don't pick an ad that has a totally different look and tone than the rest of your site; make sure the writing and images complement—and don't detract from—the overall effect of your site.

# Creating Links Within Text

The best way to use affiliate marketing is to create new, keyword-rich content that contains reviews or references to the affiliates you're promoting. To do this, you would simply join CJ.com (as outlined above), then copy the "text only" referral links from the list of options offered by advertisers, and put them in your site. Many people do this in the form of "reviews," or articles that highlight the advertisers' products.

This helps your site by:

▶ **Providing additional text links you can seed with keywords, and adding to your own credibility.** An example of how this works: "The Bugaboo stroller is by far the most comfortable one for my baby, and offers the most options when it comes to flexibility. Highly recommended by first-time parents for ease of use." In this example, the words "Bugaboo stroller" would take your users over to a baby store where they would be offered a discount, and you would get a commission when they make a purchase. This sentence also has the advantage of containing the popular keywords "Bugaboo stroller," "first-time parents," and "baby."

▶ **Adding value to your customers.** You are essentially endorsing this product or site, and since you know it will appeal to your users, this might be just the encouragement they need to visit that site, sign up, and buy that other person's product.

▶ **Generating more income.** Commissions and referral fees provide additional income streams from your site.

▶ **Keeping your site clean and focused.** By placing links within the content itself and by not cluttering your site with banner ads, you encourage the user to focus totally on your site and your content and nothing else.

Users think of embedded links much differently from the way they think of traditional banner ads. When a link to another site is incorporated into your content, users assume that you are essentially endorsing that other product, service, company, or information. Even if the other site provides the actual text, how you then present it in your site—for example, where you place it in your site and the other content you surround it with—affects how users will perceive that other brand. By the same token, when you create the text into which the link is embedded, how that brand is perceived by your users depends not only on where it is presented on your site but also on the quality of your writing.

As an example, let's look again at the South Beach Diet text link: "The South Beach Diet was originally designed for heart patients, and then was so effective at lowering people's cholesterol and keeping weight off that it became an internationally bestselling book, a line of food, and a hugely popular website." Every time the South Beach Diet is mentioned, the reader has the option of visiting the South Beach Diet site, learning more about the diet, and signing up for a membership. If readers do this, the nutritionist gets paid for the referral. Making the link clickable also raises the nutritionist's keyword index and page rank with search engines.

# REAL LIFE >>
## *Bob Gets Some Advertisers*

RAPIDLY BECOMING AN Internet expert, Bob joins Commission Junction and browses the huge index of advertisers. He notices that Petscriptions will give him a percentage of sales of prescriptions for pets, like Frontline. Since Petscriptions appeals to Bob's target audience but doesn't directly compete with his business, he can comfortably add this element to his site. He decides to incorporate into some of his informational articles a mention of Petscriptions products his customers need anyway.

I recommend that Bob take the text-only referral links from Petscriptions and embed them in his informational articles. That way, people who might leave the site do so when they're in the middle of a fascinating article they're reading, insuring that they come back for more. Now when people read Bob's articles on preventing Lyme disease or training their new puppy, they can actually go right over to Petscriptions and order the proper anti-tick medication. His users appreciate the reference and the ability to take immediate action from the article, and Bob appreciates the 10 percent commission he gets when they place their orders.

Bob is also interested in putting up some Google text ads on his site. I encourage him to try it out, to see how the ads affect his conversion rate. If more people are loving the new content, reading the blog, and buying the biscuits, some relevant AdSense ads shouldn't be a problem. If his conversion rate goes down (meaning he's getting less people actually completing sales), it'll be easy for him to pull the ads off. For now, Bob and I split the difference with a half-size AdSense box that isn't competing with the main elements of the site. This will give users the chance to glance at the ads, but won't totally overpower them.

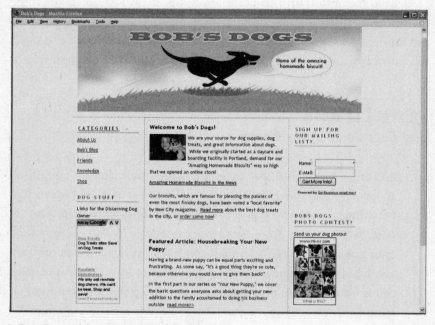

Built on Typepad, banner design by Miss Mary K.

Bob now has two new income streams from his site, and he's happy with how easy it was to incorporate them into what he'd already built. Pretty cool! Later, when he starts sending out a newsletter to his brand-new list of subscribers, we'll go over putting the affiliate marketing text links in the newsletter copy as well.

# 13 | Hone Your Homepage, Test Your Site, and Go Live!

Your homepage is your best shot—often your only shot—to convince users that you've got the right stuff . . . in ten seconds or less. Get this right, then test your site a little more, and you're good to go.

**B**y now, **I** hope you're feeling good about the direction your site is going. It's almost go time! By the end of this chapter you'll be launching your new site. Before we hit the button, though, I want to talk about the first thing your new (and repeat) visitors are going to see when they get to your site: your homepage.

Your homepage provides a quick glimpse of what your whole site is about, so it has to be concise, well organized, and compelling. Otherwise, users will never know all you have to offer. Experts have been struggling for years to come up with an accurate analogy for a homepage, including calling it a company's online lobby, billboard, brochure, calling card, and storefront. In reality, a homepage is all these things, but much more. In today's world of "first impressions are everything," on a homepage you have five to ten seconds to capture users' attention and clue them in to what you have to offer. In those few make-or-break seconds, users decide whether your site is really "for" them and whether it's worth sticking around a little while longer to check you out. There is no opportunity to counter a negative impression or to clear up any confusion. Everything has to be perfect.

No pressure, though.

Probably the most difficult part of proper usability design is striking the right balance on the homepage—conveying the right message in the right way. So it will likely take some trial and error before you work out all the kinks. Thankfully, the Internet, unlike traditional advertising, can be rapidly and inexpensively changed if you find something isn't working.

## Why This Discussion Is Last

Contrary to popular belief, it is usually not a good idea to start by building the homepage of your site and then work backward, creating the site as you go. It is much more effective to develop good content and to build solid information architecture first—and then, once you know what you're putting on the site and in what configuration, to design the homepage. Since the homepage is command central (that is, the platform from which all other pages on your site derive), it is much easier to change a single page that isn't working than to go back to the homepage and rework the whole site from that point forward. The good news is that when you take the time to get your materials, your blueprint, and your structure together first, the homepage (the façade) usually falls into place fairly easily.

## The Making of a Good Homepage

Now is a good time to go back to your Top Five Sites analysis to see what those sites did well on their homepages (and hopefully to borrow some good ideas from them). Keep in mind that although your homepage need not have all of the features of your favorite sites, the more closely you follow their examples, the better. Remember, a good homepage will:

- ▸ Be sleek and impressive, but not so sleek that users can't find everything they need without going deeper into the site. In other words, if I go to your site, I should be able to "get" it and to pretty much know where everything is before I make the choice to click anything, to explore, or to search. This is what is meant by intuitive design.

▸ Engage the user and clearly communicate the purpose of the site (preferably with a good tagline).

▸ Communicate the brand via the logo and tagline, without hitting the user over the head with slogans or with a slew of company-specific copy. In other words, you don't need your whole "About Us" text right on the homepage. Your brand should speak for itself, via the logo and tagline, and the design aesthetic you've chosen for your site. Don't feel like you have to overexplain.

▸ Provide enough content to engage users and to convince them that you know what you're talking about, but not so much that the user feels overloaded.

▸ Feature action items, such as an email opt-in (for a newsletter or offering) that will enable you to build up your subscriber list of interested people, a way for users to become a member (if you run a subscription site), or a button connecting people to your featured item and encouraging them to order it now, either through text or a button. Chances are good that if you don't give them something to do right away, they'll choose the obvious option—they'll go away and do nothing.

▸ Include a personal component to which users can relate—preferably a photograph of a real person (experts call this your "smiling lady"), but at least a quote from someone who has used (and liked) your product or service (refer back to Chapter 11). Ideally, you'd want a combination of smiling people and their personal stories, relating to your product or service. Putting stories or quotes from real people right up front on the homepage is an excellent way to engage new visitors and build trust, right off the bat. In the world of the five-second attention span, you need all the help you can get to make a good first impression.

Add all these elements together, stir, and voilà! You've got a great homepage. Here is an example of a well-designed homepage. Castle Hill Investments, a real estate brokerage firm in Austin, Texas, follows all the rules and presents the design elements in a simple, appealing format.

## Castle Hill Investments
*www.castlehillinvestments.com*

This site features engaging, professional language and clear contact information that compel the user to action. Action items give interested users something to do right away. Quotes from current clients instill faith in interested users, while the simple, clean design impresses potential customers. Castle Hill does a great job of engaging users with intelligent content, real stories and quotes, and "action items" for them to do. Whether or not a first-time visitor to the site actually wants to buy real estate in Austin right at that moment, by the time they leave they at least feel like they've taken the first step toward investing in some property.

Engaging content, good design, action items—easy, right? Okay, so it's not quite that simple to include all the essentials in your homepage and to make sure it meets its goal. But the following steps will give you a running start.

### *Decide on Your Homepage Goal*

The goal for the homepage is essentially whatever you want your users' first impression of your site and your business to be. By now, hopefully, you've decided on the goal for the site itself—for example, "I want people to buy my product," or "I want people to use my service," or "I want users to think I'm an expert in my field," or "I want to create a community of people who use my site (or product or service)," or even "I want to display photo albums of my kids playing soccer."

Before you start working on the homepage, take out your goals for the site, which you probably developed when you were defining your target audience (back in Chapter 2) and what you want them to do on your site, and start thinking about how the homepage can help you achieve those goals.

For instance, if one of the goals for your site is to sell more consumer electronics, the goal of the homepage might be: "To create the impression that my store is a trustworthy source of electronics, to compel customers to make a purchase and to become repeat customers."

For the Castle Hill example, the goal of their homepage is clear: They want you to be impressed with their company, look at listings of available real estate in Austin, and contact them when you're ready to buy. They know this is a big step, so they clearly list contact information (if you have questions), testimonials from other people, and impressive sales statistics from previous years (so you'll know they're not small potatoes), right there on the homepage.

By revisiting the goals for the users of your site and then constructing your homepage accordingly, you can positively impact your bottom line from the very beginning. People are going to come to your site for many different reasons, from wanting to learn more about your company, to searching for contact information, to buying a product. By making sure the site is inclusive of the above elements, you'll maximize your chances of turning every visitor into a customer.

### Make Your Homepage Distinctive from Other Pages

Although the overall look of your site should be consistent from page to page, make sure the homepage is a little different so that it can be distinguished from the rest of the pages on the site. I like to accomplish this by including some kind of "welcome" message, however small, on the homepage, so that users know that they've arrived at the destination, and feel comfortable enough to start looking around in this brand-new place. Even if you accomplish this by merely writing the word "home" on this page and no other, you've got to give your users an anchor point where they can start. Not doing this might cause users to feel lost within your site, and you know what happens when users have a bad online experience. If they can't even get past your homepage without feeling lost and disappointed, well, you can guess what their next step is going to be.

# Create a Good Tagline

If you haven't already done this in the design and/or writing phases, now is a good time to create a tagline for your site. If you don't already have one for your business that you can use on the website, start with something involving your service offering. If I were writing a tagline for Bob's Dogs, for instance, I'd suggest something like "Your neighborhood source for all things dog," just to make sure I made the point that Bob's is a down-to-earth kind of store with a large variety of dog things. To write your own tagline, first focus on what exactly your business does. Are you a "unique source of traditional Native American jewelry"? Maybe "the best barbecue sauce you've ever tasted, or it's free"? Or perhaps you're simply "the best information source for serious dieters." This might be the tagline you use for your business in general, for example in your brochures and on your business cards, or it can be a different tagline, as long as it fits your brand. It is fine to be creative with the tagline, but more important to be clear and concise. Also, you don't want the tagline to be clichéd, overly cutesy, or pretentiously clever. The fastest way to find your tagline is to take the best thing you offer and lead with that. Once you have a few options (or if your business or brand is already well known), you can start getting more inventive, like the businesses I've listed below.

Here are some examples of good taglines:

**iStock Photo (www.istockphoto.com):** "The new era in royalty free stock photo images"

**CNET (www.cnet.com):** "Bringing tech to life"

**Office Depot (www.officedepot.com):** "Taking care of business"

**Vista Print (www.vistaprint.com):** "Best printing. Best price."

**HomeDepot (www.homedepot.com):** "You can do it. We can help."

A good tagline for your business belongs in all of your marketing materials, and it's great to have it on your website as well, just to establish brand consistency and easily communicate who you are and what you're about. If you've got a tagline, use it!

# The Community Factor

In my opinion, the one thing that separates the more successful websites from the less successful is the use of personal stories and community, which we covered in Chapter 11. If you are taking only one of my examples and implementing it into your site, please let it be this one. The personal story can be the thing that makes all the difference.

Whether it's in the form of short testimonial quotes (as in the Castle Hill example), profiles of real nurses (like those on the DiscoverNursing website), or a photo contest where people can submit pictures of themselves, real people make the Internet more human, and they'll make your homepage more engaging.

If there is any doubt in your mind regarding the value of the personal story, please refer to the website of a company called LifeLock (www.lifelock.com), which provides protection against identity theft and fraud. Now, this is a subject that most everyone finds terrifying—identity theft is on the rise, almost everyone knows someone to whom it's happened, and it has the potential to ruin your life. In this way, LifeLock doesn't have to work very hard to sell you their actual product, since we're all motivated by fear. But, through the use of high-quality photos of real people along with compelling stories about how this company saved them from identity theft, they differentiate themselves from the numerous other companies offering this service. By including a slide show of real-life customers, LifeLock literally sells itself.

Generally speaking, the more technical your site or product, the more you'll need the personal/community factor, as in the example of LifeLock—an identity theft protection service (technical) that sells itself through the use of real identity theft stories and pictures of real people (personal). Personal stories and quotes from real people help communicate the user-friendliness of your products, company, and site . . . much like word-of-mouth advertising. When users read how real people benefited from doing business with you, it builds their trust in you, makes them relate to you on a personal level and want to do business with you too. Using stories and quotes can increase the length of users' visits to your site, improve your conversion rates, and increase your sales.

If you have one or more of these elements and you're happy with how your homepage presents itself, then you are ready for the final step: Test, then go live!

# Test, Then Go Live!

Prying eyes want to know: Is your site ready for the world?

At the end of your site design/redesign process—before the new site officially goes live—you'll want to conduct a few tests to pinpoint those flaws that only a systematic assessment is likely to reveal. Outside testing is a very important part of website development that is too often overlooked. As helpful as it is for you and your friends to look at your site with a critical eye, as we did in Chapter 1, those honest opinions are inevitably somewhat biased and rarely catch every hitch and hiccup. The main purpose of formally testing your site is to get some fresh perspective on it. After all, by now you've probably worked on it so much you can't see the forest for the trees and are likely to miss flaws that would be glaringly obvious to someone looking at your site for the first time. At this point, uncovering any hidden flaws that might be lurking on your site requires the objective scrutiny of several pairs of critical eyes.

Really, though, testing right before launching a new site (or relaunching an old site) should be considered essential, and testing of any kind at any time during the life of a website is always money well spent. Bottom line: Testing is invaluable, and it should be a line item in budgets of all sizes.

## Focus Group/Usability Testing

Many people ask—"Should I repeat the tests I did on my old site now?" This is the testing from the beginning of the process (as outlined in Chapter 6). You don't have to do these tests now if you're totally confident in your site, but as I've said before, I don't think you can ever get too much feedback. If you have the budget and feel like you want to run your new site by a few users who match your targeted demographic, then by all means, return to Chapter 6 and repeat the focus groups and/ or usability tests. Just make sure you allocate additional time and budget for changes, in case your group comes up with another round of things to tweak on your site. For this reason alone, some people get their site to a place where they're satisfied and skip the additional focus grouping/usability testing. If you're happy with where your site is now and confident in its design and functionality, then by all means move on to the next set of tests: quality assurance testing, where you make sure everything works, from the links to the "Contact Us" page. Whereas usability testing addresses the larger issues of the website, quality assurance testing is more of a functional, nuts-and-bolts testing, a kicking of the website's tires before you take it out on the road.

## Quality Assurance Testing

The ideal time to do a quality assurance (QA) test of your site is right before the launch. The purpose of a QA test is to go through the entire site, word by word and task by task, to find and repair any and all content and technical errors—such as typos, misspelled words, fuzzy images, overlapping text, coding errors, broken links, misdirected pages, shopping carts that don't work, and the like. QA testing usually calls for a team of skilled professionals who are trained not only to find site errors but also to document, replicate, and determine the cause of them. In other words: They're expert diagnosticians. QA people rarely fix the problem, but they usually know what it is, how it occurred, and how to prevent it.

To find a QA person or firm, I would suggest going back to our old friend, Craigslist. You would look under "Resumes" at the bottom, and then search for "QA." There you will find a list of technical folk who will be happy to put your site through its paces—for a price.

If you can't afford to hire a web QA team or even a single QA specialist, I suggest you send your ten smartest friends (all the better if one or more of them has some hands-on web design or construction experience) on a bounty hunt for QA gaffs on your site. Offer a reward, like $5 for every mistake found, or offer an incentive, such as taking whoever finds the most errors to dinner. Believe me, whatever you give your friends to find those mistakes will save you an exponential amount in lost business should, say, your shopping cart dump someone out in the middle of a transaction, your "Contact Us" button lead to nowhere, or the "Buy Now" link to your bestselling product not work.

Ask your QA team to tell you exactly what they were doing (or trying to do) when the error occurred (or the site crashed). What operating system were they using? What browser? What was the exact series of steps they took to create that error? Were they able to replicate it? The reason for these questions is simple: You're looking for major errors within the site that are likely to trip up other users, not "ghost in the machine" type stuff that can only be replicated once in a blue moon. Your goal with any kind of QA testing is to work out the site's major bugs before they start to frustrate real customers.

## Budget All-in-One QA Testing

In an email explaining that you are looking for feedback on your new site, send your URL to everyone you think might really check it out and give you honest opinions. Ask people to click through the site and report back to you their overall impressions and, specifically, everything that doesn't work, that they don't like, and that they really like. Ask them not to hold back.

Warning: This exercise is not for the faint of heart. You might hear some things that are too candid for your taste. Remember, the user experience is based on actual use and comprehensive feedback, so you're not looking for a bunch of yes people.

Here are some of the key things to ask:

1. Click all the links on the site. Do any of them not work?
2. Could you find what you were looking for in a reasonable amount of time?
3. Please state the objective of this website, based on your impression.
4. What's your overall impression of my business, based on this website?
5. Would you have faith in this site to complete a transaction?
6. Was there any point at which you hit a dead end, meaning you got lost, couldn't turn back, or forgot what you were doing? If so, please describe where you were during this exact moment.
7. What browser were you using?
8. What operating system were you using?

My advice: Do whatever you can to get friendly eyes to catch mistakes before you start submitting your site to the search engines (which you'll do in Chapter 16). How would you feel, knowing that your site flunked Google's inclusion test (also known as a "spider") because of some broken links that you could easily have caught?

Following are the main things to double-check. (Personally, I think you can never check these too many times before a launch. Even if your QA team has signed off, do yourself a favor and click all the links in your site. You might find something that doesn't work, or doesn't work the way you wanted it to. Either way, you saved yourself money.)

Functionality:
- Do all of the links work? If not, go back and fix them.
- Is it easy to find your contact info? Does the contact email work? Send yourself a test email just to be sure.
- Is everything spelled correctly? If not, go back and fix errors.
- Are my most popular products easy to find? If not, go back and add some clearer links to your homepage.

Usability:
- Is my site free of the egregious usability errors that were discussed in Chapter 7? By now, I'm hoping you've gotten rid of broken links, anything that pushes a download right from the homepage, music, and other annoying things. But here's another chance to review. Please take this stuff off if you can. It's not helping you, and I don't want to see you spend money advertising a site that's going to hurt your business.
- Is it easy to find things on your site? If not, go back to Chapter 8.
- Do I have a good amount of engaging articles/content that contain my keywords? If not, go back to Chapter 3 and Chapter 9.
- Does my design match my intended target audience? If not, go back to Chapter 10.

If you can confidently answer yes to all of these questions, then it's time to relaunch. Go ahead and "publish" your new site (if you haven't already), or move the new files over to the live server, or give the green light to your web development person. However you're making the new site live, now is the time.

# REAL LIFE >>
## *Bob Hones His Homepage*

AFTER I SHOW Bob examples of other companies that got their homepages right, he and I talk about what's going to go in the coveted center spot of his homepage. Since Bob has used TypePad to make his site, most of the elements on his homepage are going to be consistent for every page in the site (with the exception of the content that appears in the center when people click on specific sections, and the "Store" link, which launches a separate storefront). On the homepage Bob just needs to add some engaging stuff that will welcome people to the site. It would also be nice if they were given an opportunity right away to buy his bestselling product, the Amazing HomeMade Biscuits.

He's identified his target audience (people in their twenties and thirties who love their pets like children), and he's clear about what he wants them to do. His goals for first-time visitors to his homepage are, in order of importance to Bob, that they:

1. Recognize his store as a great resource for dog products and information, and think, "Hey, this is a site I'd like to come back to."
2. Join the mailing list for future updates.
3. Buy the dog biscuits.

Like all small business people, Bob wants to boost his sales. The best way for him to do this is to build up his "user base" of people who are interested in his products and articles. He's got his "sign up now" box in place, and he wants to steadily grow the number of people who are buying products from him (as well as grow the audience for his eco-friendly pet blog). We start with a "welcome" message which lets users know where they are. I also recommend putting a sales-focused action item right in the center—for now, he'll put up the first couple of lines from an article that mentioned the Amazing HomeMade Biscuits, which will include a link to buy them.

Bob's homepage (and really, his whole site) reflects his overall brand. It has a clear message, which is communicated by the banner and tagline, and it gives users (first time or otherwise) things to do when they're clicking around. It has a "welcome" message so that people know where they are when they hit the site, and the clearly marked categories are intuitive, so people know where to look if they want to, for example, read articles or buy something.

Bob's homepage incorporates the "personal" element through the use of both a photo contest and a blog (which Bob promises to update at least a few times per week). All in all, a first-time visit to Bob's homepage will be a great experience, and users should want to come back again and again.

The final step in Bob's website transformation (and yours) is to put it to the test. Bob is thrilled with his new site, and happily puts it through my Quality Assurance Checklist. He sends it out to the group of friends and family members who totally hated his old site back in Chapter 1, and is thrilled with the feedback that comes back:

"Wow, Bob—this site is awesome!"

"I just bought some biscuits!"

"Sorry I took so long to answer back—I was reading your article about dental care for dogs, and lost track of time. So interesting!"

He does get one comment about a broken link in one of his articles, and so we go back and fix that. Overall, though, Bob's revamped site passes his "budget all-in-one QA testing" with flying colors, so he's comfortable relaunching.

Since he's using TypePad, Bob is going to have to go into his domain registrar (in this case, GoDaddy.com) and tell it to "point" toward the TypePad site. TypePad has an extremely clear set of instructions on how to do this in their "Control Panel" section. On the TypePad side, Bob just needs to:

Go to Control Panel > Site Access > Domain Mapping.

Click "Begin Here: Map a Domain Name."

Enter his website's URL.

Bob will then need to go over to his hosting service (in his case, also GoDaddy.com) and set his DNS (domain name system) settings so that they point to the TypePad account. On the GoDaddy side, they have an excellent set of instructions on how to do this, and twenty-four-hour tech support if he needs help any step of the way.

Once this is done (in some cases, updating these settings can take twenty-four to forty-eight hours), he'll just need to make the site "live" on the TypePad side. From then on, everything he enters through TypePad will appear live on his "Bob's Dogs" site. Easy!

So that's it for revamping (or creating) your site. Good job! I know, it's been a lot of hard work and new information, and your head is probably still swimming. But hopefully by now you've got a new and improved version of your site up and running, or you've started a strong and effective brand-new site and you're ready to move on to the next phase—promotion!

# Marketing, Search Engines, and Advertising

**A**nd now, the last part in the "total website domination" plan—marketing and promotion. Now that your site is all that it can be, the challenge is to get as many people as possible to come and check it out.

This is the part where we open the floodgates, and try to get everyone who uses the Internet (or at least everyone who is interested in what you're selling) to come on over. We'll talk about how to get you into the search engines (and get you ranked as highly as possible). We'll also cover search engine optimization (beginning and advanced), search engine submission, pay-per-click advertising, and other ways to promote your site.

By the end of this section, I guarantee you will have learned a thing or two, and you'll have some killer ideas for attracting more people to your site.

So let's get started. We have so much to talk about!

# 14

# Rev Up for Search Engine Optimization (Beginner)

Strategic use of keywords in content will give your site the fuel it needs to boost your search engine rankings.

**A**h, **search engine** optimization. Go into any coffeehouse in San Francisco, and you can probably find two or more "techie" types debating the finer points of this subject. The art and science of search engine optimization (SEO) can be a website rabbit hole/time-waster, and for that reason, I'm going to try to get us in and out of this subject in two chapters or less. If you want just the basics, read this chapter and follow the steps. If you're more brave (and perhaps even want to join the debate), roll up your sleeves and go to Chapter 15. That is where it gets a little complicated, and I'll do everything I can to keep it simple along the way.

The next step in your website improvement process is to make sure your site is properly "optimized," so that when you submit it to the search engines (in the next chapter), it ranks as highly as possible. For this, you'll need the keyword list that we constructed in Chapter 3. Now we're going to use that list to put those keywords inside your site to make it even more magnetic to search engines. For the record, I consider search engine optimization to be an effective way to get people to a site that is already strong on usability, content, and conversion rate. In other words, don't submit until your site is strong and functional. In plain terms, you wouldn't have a dinner party until you felt like your house was up to snuff. You never get a second chance to make a first impression, so just take some time to make sure you're confident about your site's strength, before you go submitting it all over creation. Once your site is search engine–friendly, you can begin the process of submitting and registering it with the search engines.

So bear with me. This won't take long, and you'll thank me in the long run.

To define the term (and really, a whole industry), search engine optimization is the process of making your website as "friendly" to the search engines as possible, so they will list your site highly (preferably on the first page) in their search results. When your site is "weighted" favorably in the search engine, people will find it when they conduct searches, they will buy your products, and everything will function as it should.

So what's the big deal? Let's start from the beginning.

# What's a Search Engine?

A search engine is a particular system that allows you to search and find sites on the Internet. The most popular example (or, at least the one that most people ask me about) is Google, but there are many others, including Yahoo!, MSN, Dogpile, AltaVista, and new ones springing up every day.

## How (We Think) They Work

A search engine is a powerful computer information system that enables Internet users to search the web for websites that are relevant to whatever topic the user specifies by typing the keyword (or phrase) into the search engine's search field. For example, if you type the words "dog food" into Google, you will be presented with millions and millions of relevant results. Having a good search engine ranking (meaning your site shows up as one of the top results) is definitely an important part of the overall health of your website.

## How Can I Tell Where I Am Now?

Good question. Remember Google PageRank, from Chapter 5? Now would be a good time to revisit where your site stands in the rankings. If you've just relaunched your site, maybe your PR (PageRank) has already gone up. Google PageRank is a good indicator of where your site stands in the vast network of sites at Google's disposal. At least Google PageRank is a measurement of whether your site is getting search-engine stronger. Check it often. Go to http://toolbar.google.com to get started if you haven't already.

## How Do I Get to the Top of the Results?

In my experience, people searching the Internet don't usually go beyond page 2 of the search results, since relevance falls off a lot after that, and you've probably already got twenty-five sites that are offering what you need. So how do you make your site float to the top of the pile? That, my friends, is the million dollar question. Since the search engines use a combination of factors to "rank" your site, you need to make sure you've created a user-friendly site with good content and well-placed keywords that will make your "rank" go up.

Here's how your site gets into the search engines:

1. You submit it yourself or use a company to submit it for you.
2. The search engine "spiders" your site, which means they send a little program over to look at your site's code. This is when it becomes very important that your site is not built entirely of Flash, does not consist of one big image, and is not in frames or anything else that might prevent the spider from "reading" the site. You want to put as few obstacles as possible in the way of letting the search engines spider your site. If your site is "invisible," so to speak, it will never make its way into the search engine rankings.
3. Based on more than one hundred factors, the search engine ranks your site, and it starts appearing in search results whenever someone uses the search engine to search on your keywords.

Sounds pretty simple, right? Great! Now, get out your keyword list from Chapter 3, and let's get started.

Here is my basic search engine optimization formula:

smart content + well-placed keywords + basic submissions + time = search engine ranking

That's it—the big secret formula. Make something good, be smart about where you put the right words, put it on the radar of even the most basic search engines (which I've outlined below), update it frequently, and wait. Before long, the search engines will pick you up, and you'll start getting customers through "natural traffic."

Listen, I'm not saying a $500,000 budget isn't going to help your search engine rankings at all. There are some really good advertising programs where you can pay to get people to come to your site (which is different than the affiliate or advertising programs we've covered previously), and we'll get to those in Chapter 17. It is also generally true that the more you spend on traffic-building strategies, the more successful you will be in increasing traffic to your site. However, no matter how great your site is and how much money you throw at increasing your exposure with search engines, if your site is new or you are submitting it to search engines for the first time, it's going to take a little while before your site takes root with the search engines, people become aware of it, other sites start linking to it, and so forth.

Think of it this way: When you plant a tree in your yard, you have to wait for it to grow to its full height and breadth. You can select a species well suited to your environment, plant it in the ideal place on your property, give it the right amount of water and all the right nutrients, stake it and prune it to give it definition, keep the kids from hanging on it and the varmints away from it, and even talk nicely to it (hey, some experts swear this works), but that alone will not make the tree grow. Once you've done your part, the rest is up to Father Time, and all you can do is be patient and wait.

Fortunately, there are some things you can do to give your site a running start on the mad dash to search engine optimization. So grab your keyword list from Chapter 3 and let's focus on something you can control: where you place keywords on your site.

## SEO: Smart Content

We covered this in Chapter 9, but it's so important that we're going to revisit it for a moment here. Once you've defined your primary and secondary users and created your keyword list, you should incorporate those keywords into your content. Ideally, you should do this as you're writing the content for the site, as discussed in Chapter 9. But if you have already built your site and now want to improve its search engine performance, adding keywords to your content will put you well on your way to a winning search engine strategy.

Take a look at your keywords list and make note of the most popular words on your list. From now on, when writing or updating content for your site (or having others do it), make sure to include at least your most important keywords in the content. For example, the top keywords for a site that sells maternity and baby clothes might be "baby," "baby clothes," "maternity," "maternity clothes," and so forth.

Include at least one of your top ten keywords in every:

▶ Title
▶ Headline
▶ Paragraph (if not sentence)

If you're finding it difficult to fit your keywords into your existing content, try writing some new articles that focus on one or two keywords (see Chapter 9 for a review on this). Since you should be adding new content on a regular basis anyway, you will have many opportunities to add keywords, and on a fairly frequent basis. I also suggest that you look over your site from time to time to ensure that you're using your keywords enough. There are several good "keyword density" analysis programs that can tell you how keyword rich your site is overall (see page 208), and you can use the results to add some more "smart content" accordingly.

Adding keywords to your content might seem like a no-brainer, but maximizing your keyword density without making your writing sound ridiculous or pretentious is actually a tricky balancing act. When in doubt, always err on the side of better content and fewer keywords. Remember: The objective is not only to get people to your site, but also to engage them in a positive way while they're there, so that they'll convert to customers and come back. Otherwise, if your whole point were just to boost your search engine rankings, you could simply fill your entire site with nothing but keywords and forget about it. Right? Obviously, a site that's 100 percent keywords will be number one in all the search engine results, right?

Wrong.

This is called keyword stuffing, and it will get you banned from all of the major engines. The game is to get the words in there by posting relevant content on your site that actually addresses those subjects. The search engines can tell the difference between a page of keywords and a page of keyword-rich content, about as effectively as you can tell a good neighborhood from a very bad one as soon as you turn onto the street. A keyword-stuffed site is the Internet equivalent of a bad neighborhood—you don't want to go there.

What happens when you get "banned" by the search engines? Search engines might refuse to look at anything from your domain again, and they'll never "spider" your site again (because it's blacklisted), so you'll basically never end up on a results page again. Since it's already hard enough to rise up in the Internet ranks, definitely don't use bad business practices. You will get caught.

And how will you know if you've been blacklisted? Believe me, no one's going to contact you to let you know. But let's be honest here— if you're engaging in one of the Internet "bad behaviors" like keyword stuffing, cloaking, shady redirection, or duplicate content, and you notice that your traffic suddenly grinds to a halt or you can't find yourself in relevant search engine results, then it's happened. I won't go into the details of all the shady business practices, either those named above or the myriad others, because (a) I don't want to give you any ideas, and (b) I don't like to give airtime to that kind of nonsense, so suffice it to say that if you use your best practices, you will stay in the good graces of the search engines. If you'd like to read more about this subject, visit

Google's best practices source at www.google.com/support/webmasters (click on "Webmaster Guidelines").

How do you strike a balance between using a lot of good keywords and writing coherently? That's where the art of writing killer content comes in.

Here's an example of what not to do: "Welcome to babyclothes.com, where you can buy baby clothes. We are all things baby clothes!"

Sure, this will make your site rank better in the search engines, because the words "baby clothes" appear so frequently, but once you've attracted the potential customer, they're going to immediately recognize that you're gratuitously using keywords just to get people to your site. People can see right through this type of ploy, and it just diminishes their user experience and their confidence in you, and rarely results in a sale. Your content should not only attract users to your site, it should also engage them and satisfy their need to know (as discussed in Chapter 9).

Here's a better keyword-laced content example for the baby and maternity clothes site: "Welcome! At babyclothes.com, we've got a great selection of baby clothes and baby gifts for expectant moms."

This tagline says basically the same thing as the other one, but in a more natural and interesting way that satisfies both objectives: engaging users and using highly searchable keywords. In fact, this sentence includes the keywords "baby" and "baby clothes," as well as three additional keywords: "expectant mothers," "gifts," and "baby gifts."

As I said, it's a balancing act: using enough keywords to get noticed by the search engines but not so many that it alienates your visitors. Learning how to subtly integrate keywords into your content takes practice, but after a while, you will surprise yourself with your own cleverness.

Make sure to include keywords in your tagline, headlines, links to other sites, and titles of articles. Given the choice of using two words that mean roughly the same thing, I would recommend focusing on the one that has a higher rate of searching (which you can find by visiting the free Google AdWords Keyword Tool at https://adwords.google.com/select/KeywordToolExternal). The more keywords you can genuinely put into your site, the more the search engines will like it and the more qualified users they will drive there.

Once you're done reworking your content to add more keywords, you might want to test the site's total keyword density by visiting one of these sites (they're both free):

www.keyworddensity.com
www.webjectives.com/keyword.htm

These services are going to tell you how "keyword dense" your site is, meaning, how many times the popular keywords are showing up in your site. If you're coming up short but you know you have a lot to say on those subjects, by all means do the work of integrating those important words into your site, preferably before you put yourself on the radar of the search engines.

If your score is still low after you've reworked your content, just make a note in the future to produce more stuff with those words featured, even if it means writing a bunch of new articles. As long as you're aware that you need to start doing this, you should be fine as you create new content.

## SEO: Smart Links

This is another one of those "can't hurt to have it" items, and I actually have seen a client's Google PageRank go up noticeably after we changed his links. One of the factors that is said to affect your search engine ranking is the number of keyword-containing links your site has. Check your entire site for the words "click here" and for any other text that is linked (either internally or with a link that goes to an external site). Each of these links should contain a keyword. This is part of how the search engine knows what your site is about and how relevant it is to other sites. Here's an example of a link that does not have a keyword embedded in it: "To see tons of baby clothes, click here!"

In this sentence, the words "click here" are just a waste of a good opportunity. This sentence would be more likely to be effective in terms of search engine ranking if it read: "To see all of our great baby clothes, visit the Baby Clothes section!"

Either link would take the user to the "Baby Clothes" section, but only the second one would accomplish that *and* boost the search engine ranking, because it includes the keywords "baby," "clothes," and "baby clothes" two times each, while the first example includes these keywords only once. That's double the keyword potential.

Your task now is to rewrite all of the links on your site to incorporate your keywords.

From now on, you'll want to be more aware of keywords when you post new things to your site—include them where you can, including titles of articles, new links, what you name your photos, and of course in the content itself. Every word on your site counts, so use them wisely.

# REAL LIFE >>
## *Bob Makes His Content "Smart"*

JUST BY RELAUNCHING Bob's site with all the new content and articles (and with the words not trapped inside the design), we got his Google PageRank up to 5, so we're happy with that for now.

But Bob is armed with his keyword list from Chapter 3 and is game to find more places to use them on the site. He decides to use one of the keyword analysis tools to see how he's doing in terms of supply and demand. By running his site through one of the free keyword analysis websites (listed on page 208), he determines that he needs to add additional keywords to his content to make his site more competitive. He combs through his content, rewriting and adding keywords (but not so much that it sounds robotic, of course). He then picks his top ten keywords and writes some new articles based on them for the site. His content is coming together, his site is now a search engine magnet, and he's ready for the next step—submitting to the search engines.

Speaking of going deeper into HTML, if you're technically inclined and have a little time, go on to the advanced keyword-placement tips in the next chapter. If not, save it for later!

# 15 | Advanced SEO

If you can get to the nuts and bolts of your website (the code), putting keywords in certain areas will make it that much stronger.

**T**his chapter is for those who have the interest and wish to delve more deeply into the world of search engine optimization (SEO). It's a little complicated, and you can always come back to it if you're eager to move on to things like marketing and publicity. In order to implement these specific strategies, you'll have to know how to get into the actual HTML and edit your site. If you're using a template (like Homestead, WebSite Tonight, or anything else that generates your site for you), you will most likely not be able to change your HTML code, and you'll have to rely on the things we've covered so far, like keyword-rich content. Flag this section for the future, though—you never know when you might want to learn HTML and get really techie.

## Advanced SEO: Putting Your Keywords in the Code

Now that you've written keywords into your content, you're going to take your keyword list and put it into some key areas that most people over-look. The first step to doing this right is to make a list of your top ten most relevant keywords—words that are different from each other (so you're not accused of "stuffing") and each of which has a high rate of searching (from the keyword tools in Chapter 3). This is when "supply" meets "demand" so to speak, as you embed the highly searched words into the actual code of your website. Here are some places where you'll put the list of words:

▶ Alt tags
▶ Title tags
▶ Meta tags (including page description and keywords)
▶ Page description

According to search engine optimization theory, the more keywords you have in your site, the higher it will be ranked. If so, then taking every opportunity to insert keywords into these additional areas is an effective way to improve your ranking. That said, many people have done wonderfully with their sites without knowing how to do this. Bottom line: If you know how to do it, it's a "nice to have," but if not, just focus on increasing the amount of keyword-rich content you have on your site.

To put keywords into your site's code, refer back to your keyword list from Chapter 3 and enter the appropriate keywords wherever you want them on your site (alt tag, title tag, meta tag, or page description).

## Alt Tags

The alt tag is the little label that comes up when you put your cursor over a photo or other graphic file and leave it there.

Alt tags are primarily used by software that reads pages to the visually impaired, and most users never see them (or don't know even about them). Your alt tags are a good opportunity to describe the images on your site using keywords, to repeat any words that may be contained in other graphic files (logos, graphical titles, or headlines), and to get some more keywords into your site. Every image on your site—including headlines, banner ads, and photos you might have created in another program like Adobe Photoshop or Fireworks—has a space for the alt tag description, and you should use *all* of these. The alt tags are located next to the code for the image source.

In order to put your keywords into your alt tags, you'll need to open up your site in a program that allows you to see and edit the tags, like Dreamweaver.

## Title Tags

The title tag is the page title and description that you see at the very top of the browser page.

Many people just write the name of their site on a title tag and then use the same tag for every page, but this is a missed opportunity, as title tags are another great opportunity to use your keywords. I suggest writing a snappy, one-line description for each page. It doesn't take much effort, and it can step up your keyword density even more. Not only will this increase your search engine ranking, it will also provide users with a constant reminder of where they are in your site and what your site is about. Descriptive title tags are useful and informative to your users, and that's always a good thing. As with alt tags, you can change title tags in Dreamweaver or a similar HTML program. I suggest creating a simple page description or catchphrase that uses one or more of your most popular keywords.

While we're on the subject of page titles and title tags, there are two important things to remember:

**Don't use "the" as the first word on your page title.** Even if the official name of your company or product starts with the article "the," drop it from your homepage title tag. This is an easy way to give your website a competitive edge, because doing so will cause your site to appear higher in any alphabetical index in which it appears, including a bookmarked list. If your company is the Aardvark Store, this is going to make a big difference for you.

**Do put a title on every page.** Every single page has space for a page title, and it should be used to full advantage. Even if it's just copying and pasting the same title or short description over and over again, using these spaces is better than not using them, for sure.

## Meta Tags

In the old days of the Internet, meta tags were thought to be the secret way to rank well in the search engines. Meta tags are special HTML tags built into your pages that are invisible to the user but that carry information about the page they're on. With a little knowledge, you can add some descriptive tags to your site that won't appear on the site itself, but might make the site rank higher in the engines. Although the jury is still out on whether this remains true, it can't hurt to add some keywords to your meta tags. Meta tags can be added or changed in Dreamweaver or a similar HTML editing program, and include the description and keyword tags in the actual website code.

## Description Tag

The page description is a type of meta tag that you can insert into the code of each page. This is a 250-character (including spaces) blurb used to describe your site—and a good opportunity to use keywords. Search engines sometimes just grab this blurb for their directories, which is why it's good to hedge your bets by putting your own content in there. The page description is another often-overlooked opportunity to promote your site and use your keywords in the site.

Use Dreamweaver or another HTML editor (or go right into the HTML code of your site if you know how) to create or modify your description tag, using as many keywords as you can without stuffing.

This is the place where you put the description of your site. If your site sells baby clothes, baby supplies, gifts for expectant mothers, and any other keyword items you think are important, include them in your description tag.

There are many heated debates going on within the SEO community regarding how much of this stuff really matters, as well as discussions of new places to put keywords. If this interests you, visit Search Engine Watch (www.searchenginewatch.com), where you will be able to get all of your advanced questions answered. Search Engine Watch has tutorials, free articles, and forums where you can develop your strategy.

# REAL LIFE >>
## *Bob Takes It to the Next Level*

SINCE BOB'S SITE is made from a custom TypePad template, he won't be able to get in there and change the code himself, but he can add a simple set of keywords by going to Weblogs > Configure > Publicity, and entering his top keywords, as well as a lengthy, keyword-rich description of the site. This will automatically insert the keywords into his site's meta tags, which we'll be covering further in the next chapter. Typepad also offers a "keywords" field on every post, so he'll keep his keywords list handy and stick those in every time he adds a blog entry or new section to the site.

Should he want to get more technical, he'll need to switch to editing his site in "Advanced Templates" mode, where he can see and edit the actual HTML code of the site. Bob's not interested in going that deep at this time, so he sticks with the keywords and description in the "Publicity" section and adding his keywords to the posts. This will suit him just fine.

# 16 | Start Your (Search) Engines

"If you build it, they will come . . ." is not the case with search engines. Actually submitting your site to Google and the other big engines is the key to getting your site seen by the world.

**Finally! We've reached** the last part of the search engine process: submitting your site. By submitting to the search engines, you are basically inviting them to come and visit your site. If all goes well (and with your site being new and improved, there's no reason why it shouldn't), your site should be added to the directories of the search engines. Once your site is included in the search engines' directories, whenever someone types in any of your keywords the search engine will list and rank your site in the search results. If you haven't submitted your site yet (or if the search engines haven't found and added your site to their directories on their own), you're not listed in any of the big engines.

Contrary to popular belief, search engines do *not* search all sites on the Internet (which is why you have to submit yourself, which you're just about to do). They scan only those sites that are already on their radar, so you need to submit your site in order to get their attention. In theory, if you put up a good site and leave it there for a few years, eventually one or more of the major search engines will pick it up, just based on other people linking to it. But I'm assuming you want more control over the process than that, in which case it is much more effective to bring the mountain to Mohammed, so to speak—and put your site on the search engine's radar.

I recommend submitting your site to each of the major search engines and then joining a low-cost service to cover all of the smaller feeder engines for you. Remember: It is not wise to submit your site to any search engines until your architecture, content, design, and keyword strategies are all in good shape. Submitting too soon will do one of two things: (1) increase the chances that the search engine doesn't take your site at all, or (2) drive people to your site before you're ready to create a good first impression. But once your site is well built and your keyword density is up there, you just need to submit yourself to all the engines, and you are going to beat the pants off your competition.

## The Major Players

After you've implemented all of your SEO-smart keyword strategies and you're satisfied with your keyword density, you should submit your site to the major search engines. I recommend doing this yourself, rather than leaving it to your website host or a search engine submission service, if for no other reason than to ensure that your site actually does get added to the search engine directories. As of April of 2008, Google continued to increase its dominance of search engine traffic, going up to 67 percent. According to Hitwise.com, the most popular search engines (in order of popularity) are:

1. Google (67 percent)
2. Yahoo! (27 percent)
3. MSN (7 percent)
4. Ask (4 percent)

How, you might ask, does one get the attention of the major players? Here's the scoop on each one, in order of importance:

**Google (www.google.com/addurl).** It is free to submit your site to Google. Since this is *the* heavy hitter of the Internet, it's worth doing whatever it takes to get your site listed. It is usually easier to get Google's spider to index your site by getting a site with a decent

Google PageRank to link to yours; since the spider is already indexing that site, it will follow the link directly to yours. It's not hard to find out what another site's Google PageRank is, since you've already got the toolbar you downloaded in Chapter 5 (http://toolbar.google.com, if you want to go get it now). Just type the site's URL into your browser, and when you get there, the toolbar should tell you the PageRank.

As far as search engines go, Google is definitely the biggest (and getting bigger), so you'll want to submit your site even if you think it might already be on their radar. It's easy and free, and is a great place to start your submission process.

**Yahoo! (https://siteexplorer.search.yahoo.com/submit).** The first place to start with Yahoo! is the free submission, where you can enter your site as well as the website/feed of your blog if you have one. Yahoo! can also help you get listed faster through their Yahoo! Search Marketing program. (To use these services you'll need to become a member and pay ongoing fees.) Visit http://searchmarketing.yahoo.com for more information.

**MSN (http://search.msn.com/docs/submit.aspx).** MSN has a really good response time for indexing and including sites in its directory, and if your site isn't appearing there already, go ahead and submit it to MSN (it's also free). Once you're in the MSN directory, your site will be reviewed frequently, so having a site (or blog) that you update regularly keeps it at the top of the MSN search engine.

**Ask (http://about.ask.com/en/docs/about/webmasters.shtml#18).** Ask feeds many of the smaller engines. Prepare a sitemap using www.sitemaps.org, then follow Ask's directions in their FAQ. It's free to submit, and worth it in case you're not being covered by them as a result of being in Google.

These are the biggies the majority of users throughout the world use to search the web for goods, services, information, entertainment, or potential links for their sites. Registering with these search engines ensures that those millions and millions of users will be able to find you when they're searching for what you have to offer (provided, of course, that you've planted enough of the right keywords on your site).

# The Open Directory Project

This might be the best-kept secret and perhaps the most overlooked resource on the web. The Open Directory Project (ODP) is a free, volunteer-edited directory that feeds more than three hundred search engines, including the top ones listed previously, which means that all the biggies search the ODP for content.

What's so special about the ODP, and why do all of the search engines get their content from it? Quality results. According to the ODP website (www.dmoz.org/about.html):

> The Open Directory is the most widely distributed data base of Web content classified by humans. Its editorial standards body of net-citizens provide the collective brain behind resource discovery on the Web. The Open Directory powers the core directory services for the Web's largest and most popular search engines and portals, including Netscape Search, AOL Search, Google, Lycos, HotBot, DirectHit, and hundreds of others.

Awesome! So instead of submitting your site to hundreds of engines, some companies have found much better success submitting directly to the ODP, which is sort of like the mouth of the river. Of course, as with any other site to which you'll submit your own site, submitting merely means you're putting your site out there for review and does not guarantee inclusion. To register your site with ODP, go to www.dmoz.org (you must pick the category for which you feel your site is best suited, then enter it from there).

## *Become an ODP Editor*

Because the Open Directory Project is a human-edited directory, they are always looking for volunteer editors to review submissions. If you're an expert in your field and have some free time, I suggest applying to become an editor for that subject for the ODP. When you're submitting your site, look for the "Become an Editor" link and submit your resume. If you meet their needs and requirements, an ODP manager will contact you.

This might sound like a waste of time, but here's why you should do it. As an ODP editor:

1. You will review sites within your category for possible inclusion in the directory, including competitors' sites. This will make you extremely knowledgeable in your field and about your competition. (Remember that old saying about keeping your friends close and your enemies closer? 'Nuff said.)

2. You will have better luck getting your site listed in the ODP if you're an editor, because you'll have control over content for your section and can include your own site and the sites that you frequent. Bear in mind, I am not, by any means, telling you *not* to include your competition in any directory. Becoming an ODP editor is a great way to stay in touch with what's happening in your field and to contribute to a better Internet by reviewing sites. If you become an ODP editor and then abuse your power by excluding your competitors, you will lose your position. The ODP has a strict code of conduct.

## Using a Submission Service

After you have submitted your site to the majors (and to the ODP, if you are so inclined), I suggest you pay a service to do the rest for you. My first choice for search engine submission services is Traffic Blazer, an awesome service offered by GoDaddy.com. For a small fee, Traffic Blazer's standard service will walk you through a series of questions, perform an analysis (which you should pass with flying colors), and submit your site to all the major engines. You'll be given a username and password, which you will need to check back with them on a regular basis to see how your submissions are going.

The Traffic Blazer program has several cool features, including one that can provide you with a report showing which search engines have listed your site so far, as well as a resubmission feature (included in the basic annual fee) for resubmitting your site to search engines at regular intervals. This is an economical way to submit to a bunch of engines (and keep submitting to them). You'll be surprised at how many small search engines and directories are out there—and happy that you don't have to submit to all of them individually.

To find Traffic Blazer, go to www.godaddy.com and click on "Site Builders."

If you don't want to use Traffic Blazer, here are two other programs I've used with success:

**WebPosition Standard (www.webposition.com).** Though it costs substantially more than the bare-bones Traffic Blazer, WebPosition does more than just submit your site to search engines. They also help you with keyword research, help you understand your current success (or lack thereof) in the search engines (they call it "search engine saturation"), and let you know who's linking to you. They'll do this for up to five domains for one price.

**Dynamic Submission (www.dynamicsubmission.com).** Like WebPosition, Dynamic Submission will help you with keyword research, do your submissions (and resubmissions), and let you know what's working and not working through the use of site statistics. They also have a function that allows you to manage all of your pay-per-click advertising campaigns (which we'll be covering in Chapter 17) in one place.

The bottom line with these higher-priced services is try before you buy, because there might be more tools than you would need or would ever use. Luckily, each of these higher-priced services has a free trial, so you can play around with them for thirty days before making a commitment. If you find that you absolutely love the game of keywords, search engine submissions, and all that goes with it, then by all means, these are worth the money. I would rather see you subscribe to one of these all-inclusive services and gain knowledge *and* success for your site than to pay someone to do these things for you.

# Checking Your SEO Status

After you've submitted your site to several search engines, you'll want to periodically check to see which ones have picked up your site. You can do this in one of several ways, including:

1. Check your stats.
2. Check your Google PageRank.
3. Search your keywords (and your company name), and see where you come up.
4. Set Google Alerts (www.google.com/alerts) to see when people are talking about you.

Remember your site statistics from Chapter 5? That is one way you can look to see whose radar you're on. By going to the section called "Referring URLs" in your site statistics, you can find out which of the search engines are referring users to your site, which will tell you who knows about you.

Some statistics services can even tell you what keywords the people typed in to get them to your site. This is very cool, and sort of makes you feel like a reverse detective. Another place in the stats to find out whether you're being spidered is in the Visitor Report/Log. It is a good idea to spend some time getting familiar with the program that you're using for site statistics (whether you've decided on Google Analytics, a site stats program through your hosting company, or another one). Your statistics are the key to understanding what is working, and what still needs more attention. For instance, if you see a lot of people coming to you from MSN, but none from Google, go back and resubmit yourself to Google.

# Other Ways to Gauge Your Search Engine Success

This isn't the most precise measure of your SEO, but it will at least tell you whether you're on the search engines' radar. Periodically (but not obsessively), do a search for your company name and your own name in each of the top four search engines and any other search engines you've bookmarked, just to see where you come up. If you're like most people, you'll get a kick out of seeing your site pop up on Google, Yahoo!, and other engines.

## Search Engine Timing

Getting your site on search engine directories is not an overnight process, by any means. Google can take months to even go look at your site, and while some of the other, lesser-known engines might pick you up right away, gaining widespread search engine performance throughout the web is an incremental (and slow) process.

Just submitting your site to search engines and then waiting for them to pick you up can be frustrating. If you're selling or marketing products that will be around for the long term, it is fine to use this method and just wait it out. Of course, if you have the money, there is always somewhere to spend it, like a Google AdWords campaign (see Chapter 17).

But if you don't have extra funds to invest, here are some things you can do while you wait for the search engines to pick you up:

**Make sure your site is visible to search engines.** I mentioned this when we were discussing "triage," or fixing major mistakes made by some websites, I said it again when we were talking about design, and I'll say it again now. First and foremost, you need to make sure that when the search engines come a-callin,' there's someone home. In order for search engines to find your site and rank it favorably in user search results (the closer to number one, the better), your site must have all the attributes that search engines look for when evaluating a site to list it in their directories. Some of these are things we've discussed before (for example, the search engine must be able to see your site, so it can't be in a frame, made totally of Flash, or composed entirely of images that have words on them, also called slices). To ensure that your site is as visible as possible to search engines, it should be comprised of individual pages and not have any of the above problematic elements. As long as you can see the actual words on the site when you look at the source code (by hitting Ctrl+U), the search engines will be able to see what you have on your pages, and this is what you want.

**Find some people to link to your site.** Another criteria some search engines use for evaluation is linking, though this is becoming less and less important as more and more people have "Resources" pages that are 99 percent links. If you have one of these, I would recommend cutting it, because it's probably not doing you any good. By now, the search engines have adapted enough to know that those pages aren't "real" content, just a bunch of random links you put up. It's true, some of your site's overall success is based on how many other sites are linking back to you, but this is based mostly on quality of content (meaning, you wrote something great that everyone in the Internet wants to see, so a lot of people are linking back to that content on your site).

The bottom line on linking is: If you have an authoritative piece of content, get it out there. If you have a couple of sites with huge traffic linking back to you, that is going to help you. If you have any control over how people are linking to you, I would recommend getting them to embed your website's link in some often-searched keywords (for instance, if you sell baby clothes and you can get BabyCenter.com to link back to you, it would be great if you could get them to actually make the words "baby clothes" link to your website). Currently, a relevant keyword link back to your site is the fastest way to move your PageRank up (and move yourself up in the search engines).

But you're just starting out. How do you get people with highly ranked sites to link to you, so that the search engines rank you higher, so that more people find you? This sounds like a "chicken and the egg" type of problem, and it kind of is, but don't let that get you down. Suffice it to say that what you need is quality, original content—preferably based on and containing the keywords that people are looking for. If you don't feel like you have enough of these yet, go back to Chapter 3 to brainstorm your keyword list, then over to Chapter 9 to develop some articles. Repeat until you have what you feel is a good amount of high-quality content on your site. The amount of content you have will be specific to you, based on what you're selling and how much of an expert you want to become.

**Keep putting out the good content.** Speaking of ways to get popular sites to link to yours—the best way to get people to notice you is to do something you should be doing anyway, which is to consistently put out original content that's based on popular keywords. It sounds like common sense, but if you can write something original about a popular keyword, you're going to get more people finding you and linking to you, which is going to make your site more and more "relevant." Especially in the early days of your site, the more energy you can put into quality content (whether it's in the form of articles, interesting blog posts, photographs, discussions, or anything engaging), the faster your site will take root, get noticed, and start attracting more and more customers.

# REAL LIFE >>
## *Bob Submits His Site*

BOB SYSTEMICALLY SUBMITS his site to all the big search engines, then puts his site through Traffic Blazer to handle the resubmission process. This program will handle all of the smaller engines and save Bob valuable time by providing keyword analysis and ranking reports.

Bob wants to be proactive while he waits for the search engines, so he starts writing a lot of interesting blog posts about what's going on in the world of dogs and eco-friendly dog care. Before long, his traffic will start to go up, and this gives him something to do while he waits.

Bob also sets up Google Alerts for himself, his company, and a few for "eco-friendly dog care" and "new dog products," so he can always be in the know when it comes to new stuff. This will give him new ideas for articles and blog posts, and being in the know will help his business overall. Way to go, Bob!

# 17 | Get the Word Out to Drive Traffic Up

Don't leave it all to search engines! Use these outreach
strategies for bringing users to you.

O nce you've gotten your site ready for the search engines and submitted it all around, don't stop there. You should always be looking
for other ways to get more potential customers to your site. Don't rest
until you've got not only the amount of traffic but also the conversion
rate that you desire.

You can start being your own traffic director right now, using the strategies in this chapter. I've used all of these traffic-generating promotional
programs with various clients, with great success. Typically, I review a client's
website, site statistics, and marketing plan and then recommend one or more
of the following techniques, based on the client's business, current traffic,
and goals for the site. As you look over the list, you will find some things that
appeal to you and some things you would just never do. Pick and choose
according to what's appropriate for you, your budget, and your business.

## Pay-Per-Click Advertising

One of the most popular ways to drive up traffic is through a pay-per-
click (PPC) advertising campaign. The best known of these are Google

AdWords and Yahoo! Search Marketing. If you're not already familiar with them, PPCs are those little links (ads) that run along the top and the side of the search results for a specific keyword in the search engines. These are the same ads that would be appearing on your site if you signed up for Google AdSense (see Chapter 12), though, of course, your own text ad would never appear on your own site.

All those links on the right side of the search results are pay-per-click ads (also called pay-for-play or sponsored links). Each time a user clicks on one of those PPC links and actually goes to the site, that advertiser pays you a certain amount of money—which can range from a few cents to a hefty number of dollars per click.

Bear in mind that even though PPCs are offered by search engines, participating in a PPC program will do *nothing* to get your site in the search engine directories or improve your rank in their search results.

That said, if you have the budget for it, go into it with your eyes open, and don't expect too much, PPC advertising can be a great way to attract new customers and build your traffic. Of course, as with traditional advertisements, when you stop paying for the ad campaign, the traffic goes away. (By traffic, I mean new users; you'll still benefit from any previous visitors that bookmarked your site after finding it with a PPC ad.)

Pay-per-click advertising can be expensive, especially if done haphazardly. This is when doing keyword research and building a great, keyword-dense site really pays off. If you're interested in PPCs, first get out your keyword list (from Chapter 3) and put it to work.

In a nutshell, pay-per-click advertising works like this:

1. Decide which keyword, or keywords, you want to include in your pay-per-click advertising campaign.
2. Determine the budget for your entire PPC campaign.
3. Set a daily or monthly limit for your campaign, based on your advertising budget.
4. Create your ads. These are the words and/or images people will see when they search for the keyword associated with them. If you're advertising more than one keyword, you could use the same ad for all keywords or separate ads for different keywords.
5. Make your campaign "live."

While you're setting up your ad campaigns, you'll need to specify your "maximum cost per click," which is the most you're willing to pay when someone clicks on that word to get to your site. These are also known as "bids," though, in reality, there are no counterbids and no auction. Your bid is simply the amount of money you're willing to pay each time someone searches for that word, sees your ad, and clicks on it to go to your site. The minimum starting bid of a given keyword is based on that word's popularity; the higher the monthly volume of searches for that word, the more expensive it is to bid on. What you're actually bidding on is position, because PPC ads are given a prominent place on the screen—where users can quickly and easily spot them. Your bid, then, reflects how much you're willing (and able) to pay for your ad to show up at the top of the heap. And that depends on the value you place on the traffic that keyword will drive to your site. It is important to understand that you're paying per word and to have a maximum limit for your PPC monthly budget, but don't get too bogged down in the nitty-gritty details of "bidding per word" unless it really interests you. If it does, both Google and Yahoo! have some excellent tutorials.

Pay-per-click ad campaigns get easier to set up and manage all the time; here is where to start if you're interested in trying this out for your site:

**Google AdWords (https://adwords.google.com).** AdWords handles PPCs for Google only, though with 67 percent of all searches occurring on Google, you can't go wrong increasing your presence there. Overall, Google AdWords is very simple to set up and manage, and easy to stop if you don't see results. They also have a very clear (and free) explanation demo, which I highly recommend. If you're already a member, go to https://adwords.google.com/select/TrafficEstimatorSandbox to try out some of your keywords. Right then and there, they'll give you an estimate of what your ad campaigns might cost (you can always adjust your daily or monthly visits depending on your budget).

**Yahoo! Search Marketing (http://searchmarketing.yahoo.com).** Yahoo! Search Marketing is a little more all-inclusive, offering search engine submission services (see Chapter 15), e-commerce capabilities, and many other products in addition to the PPC ad campaigns. My one complaint with Yahoo! is that there's too much choice under the Yahoo! Search Marketing umbrella and the signup is fairly complicated, and these things can sometimes be confusing to new users who just want to set up an ad campaign and get started. If you're interested in the comprehensive services or just want to find out more, visit their site for the demos, or give them a call to speak to a representative.

If you're just starting out, I suggest that you start with a small Google AdWords campaign to get your feet wet. If you get a lot of traffic and you love the game of trying to figure out what people are searching for, then you can move on to the more complicated Yahoo! Search. Or you can start your own business doing this for other people; some people get rich doing this.

Before you go willy-nilly with your search campaigns, here are a few things to keep in mind:

▸ Some words are really popular—and really expensive. At the time of this book's printing, the average "max cost per click" for the word "mortgage," for example, was $13. That's thirteen bucks *per click*, and unless you're a big corporation with a million dollar ad budget, that is going to eat up all of your profits. While you're learning the ropes, at least, I would suggest you concentrate your advertising resources on smaller and more productive campaigns. As a rule of thumb, stay away from anything that exceeds twenty-five cents per click, as you don't want your budget to be depleted too quickly. Pay much more, and you're asking for trouble. (See next page.) This is where your huge keyword list comes in really handy, as you can spread your keyword buy over the largest area possible.

▸ Keep an eye on your site stats and conversion rates to make sure you're getting your money's worth—that is, enough click-throughs, people who click to your site and actually use it, and then, hopefully, convert to customers. If your click-through rates are low, revisit your keywords and your bids, or stop the

PPC campaign altogether. You don't want to be paying to drive too many people to your site if they're not actually becoming your customers.

## A Word on Click Fraud

At this point, you might be thinking, *What's to stop anyone from clicking on my ads, even my competitors?* The answer is, nothing, and that is one of the problems plaguing pay-per-click advertising systems. Click fraud is just that: other people (or software) intentionally clicking your links just to drive up your advertising costs, with no real intention of going to the site or becoming customers. Click fraud has become a serious problem for the industry in recent years, with some experts claiming that up to 29 percent of clicks in any campaign are fraudulent. This problem is difficult to track and to prosecute, and it's growing more rampant by the day.

Here are a few things you can do to guard yourself against click fraud:

▶ **Don't build your whole PPC campaign around one or two keywords.** Spread out your advertising across many keywords to lessen your exposure. In other words, get strategic in order to make it harder for people to scam you.

▶ **Pay attention!** Keep a close eye on your ad campaigns and report any drastic increases immediately. For example, if it usually takes the whole month to go through your monthly $500 PPC budget and you notice that you've burned through the whole budget in three days, you've probably got a problem. Contact your Yahoo! Search or Google (or whichever) representative immediately and get them on the case.

▶ **Watch your stats.** Since you've now mastered the art of calculating your conversion rate based on your site statistics and rate of sales, you're doing this on a monthly basis (I'm assuming). So you should notice if your conversion rate drops dramatically—meaning that, although the same or even a greater number of people are supposedly going to your site, fewer of them are actually converting (signing up, buying something, etc.). This could be another indicator that you might be a victim of click fraud, and you should let your advertising company know so they can investigate.

### My Secret Pay-Per-Click Strategy

This is another case where that huge list of keywords you made in Chapter 3 is really going to pay off. When you're developing your PPC ad campaign, make sure to include *all* of the keywords from your list, even the really obscure ones. By including as many keywords as possible in your PPC advertising and keeping your budget low, you'll spread out your ad budget over a wider range of words and increase your chances of driving quality users to your site. These words are also much less likely to be in use by other people, so they cost less.

Some consultants advise clients to pay the big bucks for the good words. I disagree, and think you should never put yourself in the position where you're paying a premium for any one word. In my experience, bidding on the big-money words puts too much pressure on you and your site, runs your budget out too quickly, and opens you up to a higher level of click fraud. Stick with a large number of less frequently searched, low-bid keywords, and you'll get more advertising bang for your buck while you capture more customers.

If you have the budget and can hang in there, a PPC campaign is a good way to fill the gap while you're waiting for your natural search engine traffic to build up.

## Put Out a Newsletter

As we discussed in Chapter 7 when we were talking about capturing your users (and potential users), prospective customers need to hear from you *ten times* before they convert and become customers. This is just another reminder that you should offer a newsletter, which will provide participants with a periodic reminder of who you are, and with each edition you're another step closer to converting that potential customer. If you are an expert (or anything close) in your field, you can maintain regular contact with your customers by putting out a newsletter every week, month, quarter, or whatever time period works for you. This reminds users that you exist, engages them, and drives them back to your site. Make sure to post the newsletter articles on your site as well, to help keep your online content fresh for the search engines. To get some ideas about what to put in a newsletter, go back to your Top Five Sites list from Chapter 4 and sign up for the newsletter on each one (especially DailyCandy). Pay attention to the timing, design, and content of each of those newsletters. Note what seems appropriate for your site (and what doesn't) and construct your newsletter accordingly.

The how-to of a newsletter can be handled easily in the software program you're using to capture and maintain your mailing list (such as Constant Contact, iContact, or GetResponse), as well as several free services, all of which were mentioned in Chapter 6.

To offer a newsletter in order to engage new subscribers and remind the old ones of why they signed up in the first place:

1. If you're not already, start capturing email addresses on your website. Your email subscription management software will provide the code and help with the heavy lifting.
2. Every month, get out your best new ideas and write something really engaging that you think will be of use to your target audience.
3. Load the email manager with the "broadcast" email
4. Provide a call to action in the newsletter, like a special offer or deal open only to subscribers. Note the "conversion rate," or the number of people who become your customers based on this offer.
5. Repeat as necessary and successful.

Here are some examples of sites that have engaging newsletters. I would recommend signing up for a few and taking note of what they're doing right, then brainstorming and creating your own content accordingly:

**Borders.com.** Offers a subscription-based newsletter to members with coupons and "The Shortlist," which summarizes the top picks in the store that week (including top CD, DVD, fiction and non-fiction books). Also features a "Coming Soon" section, so with one email, you're in the know *and* get coupons. What could be better?

**Oprah.com.** Members can choose to sign up for a number of different newsletters, including one on upcoming shows, one on Oprah's Radio Network, and one dedicated entirely to Marianne Williamson and *A Course in Miracles*, which is sent out at regular intervals throughout the year. Genius!

**DailyCandy.com.** Their newsletter is daily (obviously), and their subscriber base is more than 2.5 million people, eager to get their advice. With strict editorial standards for what they'll include, great art, and a wide variety of topics, they are never without something good to say.

Take the example of these sites: be succinct and relevant, offer engaging and useful content, and don't be afraid to include discounts. Your subscribers matter. Let them know that they matter to you.

## Give Away Free Stuff

If you can manage it, giving away free stuff is an excellent way to get new users to your site. People still love getting things for free, and there's always the chance that during the course of signing up for the free giveaway, people will get engaged enough to become your regular visitors. Just post a page on your site that indicates your giveaway, describe the free stuff, and explain how to get it (by signing up in the opt-in box, sending you an email, leaving a comment, and so on). Think of this as just another part of your advertising budget. You can also run this as a contest or raffle, but that does require a little bit of legal language, since technically you'll be conducting a contest. Check with a lawyer friend on this if you've got one; your contest statement doesn't have to be anything fancy, but does need to make the rules of the contest clear. Most of my clients have found that just giving something away to everyone for a finite period of time is a little easier.

Once you've decided how you're going to do your free giveaway, there are several excellent places to promote it. Email the moderators of these forums with your offer; they'll review it and post it, and then let the sign-ups begin! These sites are also fun if you enjoy getting free stuff or want to see how other companies are doing their giveaways.

www.freemania.com
www.freestufftimes.com
www.freebiereporter.com

# Stumble It

Another great way to expose your site to millions of new users is to "Stumble it," by using a website called StumbleUpon (www .stumbleupon.com). Here's how it works on the user side: You download the StumbleUpon toolbar right from the homepage, and put in your preferences. Then, when you're interested in finding new sites that are within your categories, you just click the "Stumble" button in your browser, and it will take you to a totally new site that might interest you. This new model, which they call "community-based surfing," has become so popular since its inception that StumbleUpon now has more than 6 million users. That's a lot of new people to introduce to your site.

And . . . how does this work for you, being one of the people who want to get their sites seen? It's actually pretty easy. StumbleUpon works through reference, or "sharing," so it's totally okay for you to rate your own site. Of course, the more you're rated (and recommended), the higher the chances are that you'll become a highly rated (and often referred) site in their database. As with most things in Internet Land, it does take a while for your site to "take root" in the database, but here's an interesting outcome: One of my clients averaged about 500 visitors per day. After we "Stumbled" her site and it got picked up, her traffic doubled, and actually set a record high of 4,500 visitors in one day. It's since leveled back off to about 900, but that's still a *huge* increase in her number of regular visitors. Since StumbleUpon is free (and really interesting), I would definitely recommend taking a look.

To read more about how StumbleUpon works, go to www .stumbleupon.com/about, or just visit the homepage to download the tool and start stumbling.

## Encourage Sharing

You're going to have awesome, engaging content on your site, so you'll want as many people to see it as possible, right? Be sure to include one of the cool little icons offered by either www.addthis.com or www.sharethis.com, which are easy to add right into your site, and make it simple for your users to bookmark you, send your interesting stuff to friends, recommend you to social networks like Facebook and MySpace, and favorably recommend you to "social bookmarking" sites like Digg (www.digg.com) and Delicious (www.delicious.com), where your "favorites" are shared with a large network of other users. Since there seems to be a new networking site every day, a one-stop button like this is essential, as it gives your users the tools they'll need to share your site all over the web, but limits the amount of time you'll need to spend learning about every single new site as it comes up. This saves you time while giving you the benefit of continued new advances in promotion.

## Tell a Friend

Actually, tell *all* your friends—and all your family—and all your existing customers too. The very first day your new site goes live, send an announcement email to everyone on your email list. Be sure to include a link back to the site in the email. Your existing customers will be thrilled to see that you've made changes to the site (and taken their suggestions), your family and friends will be proud of you (and maybe become customers), and when everyone on the list sees how great your new site looks, they'll start referring friends and colleagues themselves.

# Include Your URL in All Materials

Don't forget to include your URL in your email signature, your e-newsletter, and in your corporate identity (letterhead, business cards, etc.), all of your marketing materials, and any offline advertising you might run, including magazine or newspaper ads, commercials, or promotional items. Every piece of communication that leaves your office should include a link back to your website, including letterhead, business cards, brochures, press releases, and giveaways, such as pens. Every email you send—whether it originated from you, is your reply to an incoming email, or an e-newsletter—should be an invitation to return to your site. The signature portion of your email can be set up in Microsoft Outlook and similar programs (under Tools > Options > Signatures). If you have a commercial that's running, make sure it ends with your website's URL. You will be very surprised at how much your traffic goes up following the airing of that commercial.

# Get Involved in a Community

One great way to promote your site is to get actively involved in a blog or message board that already has an audience of people with similar interests. By becoming a frequent member of this community, you will start to get people interested in what might be going on over at your site. Be careful not to self-promote within someone else's blog comments or on a message board, though—this is considered bad "netiquette." The best method for this is subtlety, meaning just including a link back to your site in your comment or your profile on the message board. This will appear every time you comment. The more interesting and intelligent things you have to say on other people's sites and communities, the more you'll draw people to your own.

* * *

## REAL LIFE >>
*Bob Expands His Market*

BOB HAD NO idea there were so many options for promoting his website. First, he adds his website's URL to his marketing materials, and to the paper newsletter he sends out every month. He puts his website's URL in his email signature and on his business cards, and adds it to an ad he runs regularly in his weekly paper.

As for a pay-per-click advertising campaign to get people over to his site, Bob has about $300 a month allocated for an online advertising budget (this translates to a daily limit of $10 a day), so we get out his keyword list and set up a killer AdWords campaign, using a ton of the lower-volume (therefore, lower cost) words in order to spread his budget over as many targeted words as possible. When people search for "natural dog treats," we want them to find his site.

At the end of the first month, Bob will check the AdWords campaign to see how it's performing, and will refine it from there (trying new words and removing those that aren't performing well). He can stop or start his campaign at any time, raise or lower the budget, and see how well it's adding to his conversion rate. Going forward, Bob should keep tweaking the ad campaign until it's getting him exactly what he wants.

Bob doesn't have a lot more time after he's done these things, so I suggest he "Stumble" a couple of the articles on his site (just to get them in the StumbleUpon database), as well as adding one of the "ShareIt" icons so his users can share his awesome content with their friends.

Over time, with all of these strategies working for him, Bob's site traffic will continue to grow steadily.

Most businesses find that using at least a few of the strategies outlined in this chapter significantly increases the traffic to their sites. Try one or more for your site to find out which work well for you. You can also try to come up with a few creative ideas of your own for promoting your site, including some that are specific to your business.

Remember, however people get to your site, once they do, they should have such a seamless and pleasurable experience that they'll keep coming back for years to come.

And that's all she wrote! With that, we've reached the end of our website journey together. You've learned a ton and made some great changes, and hopefully you've learned some strategies that you can put in place right away to start growing your website and getting it out in front of the small business pack.

Before we go, though, I'll take my own advice and give you an easy-to-reference list of all the resources I've mentioned in this book.

# 18 Web Development Toolbox

Just in case you missed anything along the way, here's a whole chapter of tools and URLs for future reference.

**There are so** many good tools out there now I would be remiss if I didn't give you a comprehensive list of stuff that could help you make your site better. These have been mentioned throughout the book, and here they are, all in one place.

## Quick Website Checklist

Does your site have each of the following? If not, refer back to the chapters listed below to improve that area.

- **Clearly defined target audience and objectives.** Just by looking at the homepage, I should be able to easily discern your target audience and what you want them to do. (See Chapter 2.)
- **Clear organization.** Meaning, when users go to click on a section, they have some idea what is going to be underneath. Avoid too-clever or too-cute naming schemes, which will confuse users and make them mad at you. (See Chapter 8.)
- **Proper writing.** Every piece of writing should be an appropriate length and should have no typos or grammatical, spelling, or

punctuation errors. (See Chapter 9.) Writing on your site should also contain keywords if at all possible. (See Chapter 3.)

▶ **Interesting content.** You can do everything in this book to try to get more traffic to your site, but if you don't have interesting content (in this case, I mean the words on your site), no one is going to stay very long. Content must be appropriate and interesting to your target market. It's a fact: Content is king. Good content—not graphics, or technology, or fancy design—always wins. If you have to choose between a course in web design and a course in writing, choose writing. (See Chapter 9.)

▶ **User-friendly design.** You want your site to load quickly when potential customers type your URL into their browser. My father, who still has dial-up access, would like to say to everyone with an overly fancy, slow-loading website, "If you don't care about us, we don't care about you." (See Chapter 10.)

▶ **A well-designed homepage.** The homepage should be free of clutter and easy to figure out, with clear goals for first-time users. (See Chapter 13.)

Following is a chapter-by-chapter guide of all the tools and resources I recommend.

# Chapter 1
## *What Makes a Good Website?*

If you have no idea how to tell good websites from bad, spend a few minutes on each of the following sites and then go back to your own to look at it with fresh eyes.

## Usable Information Technology
### *www.useit.com*

Jakob Nielsen is a notable expert in the field of website usability, and although his books can be overwhelming if you're a beginner, his website provides a wealth of information. Before you make a major change to your website (especially in design or technology), I recommend perusing this site, which also includes a collection of informative articles about design and functionality.

## Web Pages That Suck: Learn Good Design by Looking at Bad Design
*www.webpagesthatsuck.com*

Vincent Flanders finds bad websites, and on his Web Pages That Suck site he explains why they're bad and how to avoid making his Daily Suckers list. Of course, this is just one guy's opinion, but he has been identifying poorly designed websites for ten years now, and he has a knack for pointing out and explaining the obvious. Spend a few minutes on this site, and you'll get an idea of what not to do and a few good laughs in the process.

## Usability.gov
*http://usability.gov*

This resource for designing usable, useful, and accessible websites is brought to you by the U.S. Department of Health and Human Services. Hey, your tax dollars paid these guys to develop this site, so why not use it for reference? The site features a handy set of checklists and guidelines for everything from design to user testing.

# Chapter 2
*Define Your Audience*

Developing user scenarios—that is, determining who your primary audience is and what they're going to do on your site—is an integral part of the development of your website.

Here are some of the sites we looked at to determine their target audiences:

**Apple Computer:** www.apple.com
**BabyCenter:** www.babycenter.com

**Barbie.com:** www.barbie.com
**BMW:** www.bmw.com
**Home Depot:** www.homedepot.com
**MTV:** www.mtv.com
**SEGA:** www.sega.com
**Toys "R" Us:** www.toysrus.com

For some helpful examples and templates on how to actually develop user scenarios, see Usability.gov's article "Segmenting Your Audience" (www.usability.gov/pubs/092005news.html).

# Chapter 3
## *Make Your Keyword List*

Use these resources to gauge the demand for your topics and content, and to build a good keyword list that you can use in your website, everywhere from the meta tags, to the articles, to the links on the site. To conduct your own research for free, use these links:

## Google AdWords
*https://adwords.google.com/select/KeywordToolExternal*

You'll need to actually sign up for an account to start using the tools, but just doing the keyword research is free.

## Wordtracker
*www.wordtracker.com*

For a much more detailed analysis, try a short subscription to this service.

\* \* \*

# Chapter 4
## *Borrow from the Best*

### FutureNow's GrokDotCom
**www.grokdotcom.com/category/conversion-rates**

Here's a website where you can see the Top Ten Online Retailers for the previous month. I would recommend bookmarking this site and reviewing it often, just to see what the Top Tens are doing.

My Top Five Sites that I think have great combinations of good design, proper architecture, and a thorough understanding of their demographics are:

**Apple Computer:** www.apple.com
**Baby.com, The Johnson & Johnson Family of Companies:** www.baby.com
**DailyCandy:** www.dailycandy.com
**Craigslist:** www.craigslist.com
**Target:** www.target.com

Here are Bob's Top Five Sites:

**The New York Times:** www.nytimes.com
**Harris Ranch:** www.harrisranchbeef.com
**eBay:** www.ebay.com
**Zappos:** www.zappos.com
**Pandora:** www.pandora.com

# Chapter 5
## *Find Your Stats*

You owe it to yourself (and your business) to have a robust system of statistics management in place, which you should check often to gauge the effectiveness of your site and any ad campaigns you have running.

Here are several good services that can help with this:

## Google Analytics
*www.google.com/analytics*

The Google Analytics program is a useful resource for measuring your site statistics. You do have to sign up for an account and know how to paste the counter into your site, but if you can figure this out, you've got a free, basic tracking system that can tell you a great deal about who is coming to your site, how long they're staying, and what they're doing.

## The Google Toolbar
*http://toolbar.google.com*

This is the little tool that you can download from Google to help you determine the strength (PageRank) of not only your site but of everyone else's as well.

## WebTrends
*www.webtrends.com*

Well known and respected in the industry, WebTrends is the gold standard for statistics measurement. WebTrends might cost a little more than the other services out there, but the information they provide is invaluable. If you're interested in using WebTrends to measure traffic, try downloading the free trial of their software from their website, and then contact them for more information and support. They will work with you and your hosting company to set up everything.

## GoDaddy's Traffic Facts
*www.godaddy.com*

I recommend GoDaddy to my clients as a hosting service—they're helpful, responsive, and very reasonably priced. If you go with them to host your site, I also recommend getting a subscription to Traffic Facts, which is the traffic measurement system they stick on your site. They do have a free statistics system that comes with your hosting plan, but the Traffic Facts system is much more detailed and robust.

# Chapter 6
*Gather Up Your Feedback and Do Some Tests*

In this chapter, we took a look at user feedback, and conducted some user tests on your site. For testing of all kinds (QA, general usability, or focus group), I suggest taking a look at the book *Don't Make Me Think!: A Common Sense Approach to Web Usability*, by Steve Krug. This short book provides a useful, boiled-down version of all the different types of testing for different budgets, without using complicated terms and getting too philosophical about the whole testing process. For user testing resources on the web, check out the following:

## All Things Web's User Testing Techniques Guide
*www.pantos.org/atw/35317.html*

## Usability.gov's Guide to Usability Testing
*http://usability.gov/methods/usability_testing.html*

Includes checklists, profile forms, and participant release forms. Thank you, Department of Health and Human Services!

# Chapter 7
*Triage*

In this chapter we talked about some of the major usability errors that you might have on your site, and how to fix them. To learn more about usability in general, visit:

## Usable Information Technology's Alertbox
*www.useit.com/alertbox*

Jakob Nielsen's "Alertbox" newsletter archive is an educational and entertaining rundown of popular usability errors from the past decade.

If your site is currently hosted on a "free" ISP (meaning you don't have your own dedicated URL yet), it's a good idea to get this out of the way before you start redesigning your site. To purchase a domain name, visit:

www.godaddy.com
www.register.com

**Email marketing/management services.** Since there are privacy and liability issues involved with collecting people's email addresses and mass emailing, I definitely recommend paying for an email marketing/management service. To start collecting email addresses on your site, try:

**PHP List:** www.phplist.com
**GetResponse Autoresponder:** www.getresponse.com
**iContact:** www.icontact.com
**Constant Contact:** www.constantcontact.com

To check your site for dead links, use one of the following:

www.dead-links.com
http://validator.w3.org/checklink

# Chapter 8
## *Nail Your Site's Structure*

In this chapter, we got into the nitty-gritty detail of how your site is organized, and made some structural changes to make it easier for your users to find what they're looking for. Here are some resources to help with that.

## The Information Architecture Institute
### *http://iainstitute.org*

The Information Architecture Institute site contains an IA Library, lists of formal and informal education in IA, and links to online communities (in case you get stuck and need to ask an expert's opinion). Also, if you find you have a real knack for information architecture, check the "Careers" section (no kidding).

To hire an information architect, go to:

www.craigslist.org
www.allfreelancework.com
www.guru.com

# Chapter 9
## *Write Killer Content*

Here we discussed writing engaging content that is relevant to your users while also being filled with keywords. Here are some resources to help:

## Nielsen Norman Group
*www.useit.com/papers/webwriting*

Extensive research conducted by the Nielsen Norman Group on how users read on the web and how to write for websites accordingly.

## Usability.gov's Writing Guide
*http://usability.gov/design/writing4web.html*

Usability.gov's short guide to writing for the web.

## HTML Writers Guild
*www.hwg.org*

The HTML Writers Guild offers several low-cost courses for developing your writing skills, including "Web Content Writing and Editing."

To hire a writer, check out:

www.craigslist.org
www.allfreelancework.com
www.guru.com

Here are two examples of writing that is at once keyword-rich, engaging, and user appropriate:

**ESPN:** www.espn.go.com
*Real Simple* **magazine:** www.realsimple.com

# Chapter 10
## *Design to Please*

Design is a field to which entire courses of study are dedicated, so don't be discouraged if the concept of redesigning your site makes you feel overwhelmed. If Chapter 10 left you hungering to try your hand at design, try the following resources:

## Usability.gov: Research-Based Web Design and Usability Guidelines
*http://usability.gov/guidelines*

## The Ten Most Violated Homepage Design Guidelines
*www.useit.com/alertbox/20031110.html*

## Web Pages That Suck: Learn Good Design by Looking at Bad Design
*www.webpagesthatsuck.com*

## Design Melt Down
*www.designmeltdown.com*

## HTML Writers Guild's Design Courses
*www.hwg.org*

The HTML Writers Guild also offers several introductory design courses. Please take one of these courses before embarking on a costly, eighteen-month web design program at an online university. You might find you've learned all you needed to know.

### *Books*

If what you really need is a how-to guide for website design, here are two books I've used with success:

*Professional Web Design from Start to Finish*, by Anne-Marie Concepcion. Simple, graphic-intensive book that clearly explains the concepts of design message and site goals, then encourages you to practice on your own.

*Robin Williams' Web Design Workshop*, by Robin Williams. No, not that Robin Williams. This is Robin Williams the designer, and this is yet another of her fine books, which focuses on teaching design with no jargon. I also recommend her *Non-Designer's Design Book*.

To do it yourself, go to:

**WebSite Tonight:** www.godaddy.com
**Homestead:** www.homestead.com
**Apple's iLife:** www.apple.com/ilife
**TypePad:** www.typepad.com (a blogging software that at the "Pro" level can be used to build websites)

To hire a designer, try:

www.craigslist.org
www.allfreelancework.com
www.guru.com

# Chapter 11
## *Get Personal*

Incorporating the "real person" or community element into your website is an essential part not only of getting more traffic, but of growing the site itself.

Here are some examples of websites that use their communities in successful ways:

**Jones Soda (photos):** www.jonessoda.com/gallery
**About.com (content):** www.about.com
**DiscoverNursing.com (personal profiles):** www.discovernursing.com/nursing-profiles

To add photos (or a photo contest) to your site:

**Flickr:** www.flickr.com
**Photobucket:** www.photobucket.com
**Photrade:** www.photrade.com

To add video to your site:

**Google Video:** http://video.google.com
**YouTube:** http://youtube.com
**MySpaceTV:** http://vids.myspace.com

## *Blogs*

Adding a blog to your site can be an effective way of encouraging repeat visitors, as people want to come back to see what you're up to as well as make comments themselves. Here are some places you can start a blog today:

**Blogger:** www.blogger.com
**LiveJournal:** www.livejournal.com
**TypePad:** www.typepad.com

Here are some examples of successful blogs (or sites that started as blogs):

**CardPlayer.com:** www.cardplayer.com
**Celebrity Baby Blog:** www.celebritybabies.com
**Dooce.com:** www.dooce.com

## Message Board/Forum Services

Adding a message board to your site can be an effective way of engaging users and encouraging them to return. You can also use your message board to learn more about your topic, to showcase your expertise in the area, and to find writers. The following can help you add one to your site:

www.boardhost.com
www.websitetoolbox.com
www.bizland.com/product/cybermessageboard.bml

Here are some examples of sites that are successfully using message boards:

**The Caregiver Initiative:** www.strengthforcaring.com
**Oprah.com:** www.oprah.com
**BabyCenter.com:** Community Discussions, www.babycenter.com/community
**Personal Development for Smart People/StevePavlina.com:** www.stevepavlina.com

## Social Networking Sites

If you're interested in building your business (or at least finding like-minded people), here are some social networking sites for you to investigate:

**MySpace:** www.myspace.com
**LinkedIn:** www.linkedin.com
**Facebook:** www.facebook.com
**Twitter:** www.twitter.com

# Chapter 12
## Add Revenue With Ads

Affiliate marketing, or the art of monetizing your website, starts with joining a network. Here are the biggest ones:

**Advertising.com:** http://advertising.com
**Clickbank:** http://clickbank.com (ebook marketplace)
**Commission Junction:** http://cj.com
**LinkShare:** http://linkshare.com

If you still have questions on marketing and advertising on your site, go to A Best Web Affiliate Marketing Forum (www.abestweb.com), look around at the different discussions, and ask questions.

You might also want to add some Google ads to your site. This is called AdSense when it goes on your site, and you can find more information at www.google.com/adsense.

# Chapter 13
## Hone Your Homepage, Test Your Site, and Go Live!

For a good reference book on this subject, I recommend thumbing through *Homepage Usability: 50 Websites Deconstructed*, by Jakob Nielsen.

This book offers insight into the do's and don'ts of website design for fifty well-known companies (some of whom changed their sites after these analyses came out).

For more information on what makes a homepage good, and how to make one:

**Research-Based Web Design and Usability Guidelines:** http://usability .gov/guidelines

**The Ten Most Violated Homepage Design Guidelines:** www.useit.com/ alertbox/20031110.html

**Web Pages That Suck:** Learn Good Design by Looking at Bad Design: www.webpagesthatsuck.com

If you have questions about the last round of testing to do before launch, I would again recommend the following books and Internet resources:

For testing of all kinds (QA, general usability, or focus group), I suggest taking a look at the book *Don't Make Me Think!: A Common Sense Approach to Web Usability*, by Steve Krug. This short book provides a useful, boiled-down version of all the different types of testing for different budgets, without using complicated terms or getting too philosophical about the whole testing process.

For user testing resources on the web, check out All Things Web's User Testing Techniques Guide at www.pantos.org/atw/35317.html.

# Chapter 14
*Rev Up for Search Engine Optimization (Beginner)*

Before you submit your site to search engines, just give it a quick test to make sure it's as magnetic and keyword-filled as possible.

To test the keyword density of your site before submitting it to search engines:

www.keyworddensity.com
www.webjectives.com/keyword.htm

# Chapter 15
## *Advanced SEO*

If you're at the advanced level of website development, meaning you can access the code and put the meta tags in strategic places, then great! You'll need an HTML editor, and here are some good ones:

**Adobe Dreamweaver:** www.adobe.com/products/dreamweaver
**Microsoft FrontPage:** http://office.microsoft.com/en-us/frontpage/default.aspx
**Coffee Cup:** www.coffeecup.com/html-editor

For more information on all things advanced SEO, visit:

**WebMaster World:** www.webmasterworld.com
**SEO News:** www.seo-news.com (also has a good newsletter)
**Search Engine Watch:** http://searchenginewatch.com (has tutorials, free articles, and forums where you can develop your strategy)

# Chapter 16
## *Start Your (Search) Engines*

Once your site is optimized, it's time to submit it to the search engines. To submit your site to these search engines, visit:

**Google:** www.google.com/addurl
**Yahoo!:** https://siteexplorer.search.yahoo.com/submit

**MSN:** http://search.msn.com/docs/submit.aspx
**Ask.com:** http://about.ask.com/en/docs/about/webmasters.shtml#18
**The Open Directory Project:** http://dmoz.org

### Submission Services

Though you'll first want to submit your site to all of the above search engines, I would recommend enlisting the help of an inexpensive submission service to do the rest of the submissions for you. This is really a "time is money" question; you want the exposure of being listed in the smaller engines, but you really don't want to spend the kind of time it will take you to find and submit to all of them yourself, when you can pay the smaller fee for the Traffic Blazer service to do both the initial submissions and the repeated resubmissions. Web Position Gold costs more, but that fee covers up to five domains, *and* they offer keyword research.

**Traffic Blazer:** www.godaddy.com (click on "Site Builders," then "Traffic Blazer")
**WebPosition Gold:** www.webposition.com
**Dynamic Submission:** www.dynamicsubmission.com

# Chapter 17
### Get the Word Out to Drive Traffic Up

Here are the major players in pay-per-click advertising:

**Google AdWords:** https://adwords.google.com
**Yahoo! Search Marketing:** http://searchmarketing.yahoo.com

### Newsletter Services

Here are the email management services that you can use to put out a newsletter:

**GetResponse Autoresponder:** www.getresponse.com

**iContact:** www.icontact.com

**Constant Contact:** www.constantcontact.com

Here are some places you can go to see examples of newsletters done well:

**Borders.com:** www.borders.com

**Oprah.com:** www.oprah.com

**DailyCandy.com:** www.dailycandy.com

## Free Stuff

People love to get free stuff, and a giveaway might be just the thing that brings tons of new traffic to your site. If you have something you can give away for free, whether it's to the first one hundred people who sign up for your mailing list, to the winner of a monthly drawing, or even a free coupon, be sure to list it on these "free stuff" sites. If one of your strategies is to give away free stuff (samples, products, or promotional items), here are some places you can go to advertise:

www.freemania.com

www.freestufftimes.com

www.freebiereporter.com

## StumbleUpon

*www.stumbleupon.com*

To start "Stumbling" your own site as well as learning about others, download the StumbleUpon toolbar.

## Encourage Sharing

To encourage your users to share the awesome content that's on your site, definitely include one of the tools to allow them to do so. Both

AddThis and ShareThis provide an easy-to-install, one-stop shop to allow your users to refer your site to social bookmarking sites, social networking sites, and much, much more.

www.addthis.com
www.sharethis.com

# Index

# About the Author

**Lori Culwell** has worked on some of the best-known websites in the world. She served as writer and content manager for several start-ups in San Francisco during the dot-com boom of the late 1990s, and as content strategist and usability specialist for US Web/CKS, where she consulted on sites for Apple Computer, Sega, Harley-Davidson, Mattel, and Sun Microsystems. In 2001, she began consulting for Johnson & Johnson and has helped create three websites for them, including DiscoverNursing.com, the number one ranked website on the nursing profession. She also consults on websites for several nonprofits and is often requested as a speaker at national conventions for organizations that wish to integrate the Internet into their marketing strategies, such as the New York Hospital Association and the Association of Academic Health Centers. The Johnson & Johnson Campaign for Nursing's Future team, of which Lori is an original member, has received the Ron Brown Award for Corporate Leadership from the White House, the Big Apple Award for Corporate Communications, and several others. Lori is the founder and president of the consulting firm Get Creative, Inc. (www.getcreativeinc.com).